BIG BAD JOHN:
The John Milius Interviews

BY
Nat Segaloff

Author of *Arthur Penn: American Director*
and *Hurricane Billy: The Stormy Life and Films of William Friedkin*

Big Bad John: The John Milius Interviews
© 2021 by Nat Segaloff

For purposes of copyright, this edition contains "substantial new material" from the original version which appeared in *Backstory 4: Interviews with the Screenwriters of the 1970s and 1980s* (CA: University of California Press, 2006) edited by Patrick McGilligan. That copyright was claimed in error by the Regents of the University of California, a mistake that was corrected by documentation confirming the copyright to the Author, who reserves all rights. No part of this book may be reproduced or transmitted in any form or by any means, electronic or mechanical, including photocopying, recording, or by any information storage and retrieval system now known or to be devised in the future, without permission in writing from the author and appropriate credit to the author and publisher. This also applies to Amazon Look Inside® and Google Books®.

Excerpts from non-auctorial interviews and other material appear under a Fair Use Rights claim of U.S. Copyright Law, Title 17, U.S.C. with copyrights reserved by their respective rights holders.

Many of the designations used by manufacturers to distinguish their products are claimed as trademarks or service marks. Where those designations appear in this book and the author and/or publisher were aware of such a claim, the designations contain the symbols ®, ℠, or ™. Any omission of these symbols is purely accidental and is not intended as an infringement. Oscar®, Academy Award®, and AMPAS® are registered trademarks of the Academy of Motion Picture Arts and Sciences ©AMPAS.

The Author attempted to source all the photos appearing in this book. Anyone feeling their photo was used without permission should contact the author with proof of ownership and it will be removed from future editions.

"At Jan-Michael Vincent Memorial, John Milius Stands Tall," by Mike Ciepley, Deadline.com, April 25, 2019, is reprinted by permission.

The story of Big Wednesday is from the Bantam Books novelization of the screenplay by John Milius and Dennis Aaberg ©1978 by The A-Team, Inc. and is used by permission of the author.

Published in the USA by: BearManor Media
4283 Express Lane
Suite 2674-933
Sarasota FL 34249
www.bearmanormedia.com

Perfect ISBN 978-1-62933-690-9
Case ISBN 978-1-62933-691-6

Cover Illustration by: Thomas Warming, ©2021
Design by: Robbie Adkins, robbie@adkinsconsult.com

BIG BAD JOHN:
The John Milius Interviews

BY
Nat Segaloff

For The Yeti
"Pain is temporary. Film is forever."

Table of Contents

Foreword vi
Growing Up American 1
The USC Film Mafia 8
Writing for Others to Direct 16
Becoming Bloodied 26
Directing Dillinger 33
The Wind and the Lion 38
Big Wednesday 43
Writing Other People's Movies 54
Conan the Barbarian 63
Red Dawn 69
Photo Gallery 76
Farewell to the King 90
Flight of the Intruder 97
Rough Riders 99
Back to Writing for Hire 105
Changing the Way Scripts are Written 115
The Value of Film 125
Hollywood Hell 130
Afterword 146
Appendix A: Filmography 153
Appendix B: Presskit Credits 154
Appendix C: Unrealized/Pending Projects 157
Appendix D: Bear's Big Wednesday Speech 159
Author Biography 161
Acknowledgments 163
Index 164

Foreword

John Milius didn't plan on being larger than life, it just turned out that way. Raised as an outdoorsman, he is an experienced hunter and marksman as well as a staunch Conservative in a business peopled with Liberals. And yet his screenplays, and the films he has directed from them, cannot be so easily pegged. His heroes are strong but have doubts; his histories are clear but complex; and he can both embrace right-wing values and detest some who espouse them. Are these traits at odds? As Walt Whitman wrote, "Do I contradict myself? Very well, then I contradict myself, I am large, I contain multitudes."

John Milius contains multitudes.

In Hollywood, where youth is valued above experience, Milius revels in being out of step. "A lot of the principles by which I live were dead before I was born," he sighed between puffs on the cigar he isn't supposed to be smoking in his two-room Warner Bros. suite. This is in 2000 as he and I begin the bulk of our formal conversations after running into each other in various cities and in assorted situations for the previous 25 years.

Below him is a parking lot full of BMWs, SUVs and Porsches, each in a space fiercely protected with a "reserved" sign. The secluded bungalow also houses the offices of producer Mark Canton, director Joel Schumacher, and actor-director Clint Eastwood. Compared to their palatial spreads, Milius's digs are positively Spartan. On his walls hang obligatory posters for his films, which include *Conan the Barbarian*, *Big Wednesday*, *Red Dawn*, and *The Wind and the Lion*. The rest of his office, which he shares with his assistant Leonard Brady, is filled with military artifacts, photos, plaques, and mementos, any of which might more properly decorate a wall in Pentagon than the cheap paneling of a movie studio. There are also shelves of books, ranging from literature to politics, that you just know have actually been read. In short, his digs are a cross between a tree fort and Elba, reflecting his demimonde status as a Hollywood insider who acts like an outsider.

"I have always been on the other side of the cultural war," the burly, bearded Milius says with relish. "I have always been an example from the beginning of that which was culturally incorrect." As to why the studio bosses resist green-lighting his personal projects, he surmises, "I think they go around and say, 'He's too much trouble' or 'I don't want to deal with him because he won't do what I want him to do.'" Regardless of trends, he remains a traditionalist. He detests "hipness" and "cool," belongs to the NRA, has a broad range of military contacts, and is politically conservative—a resume that brands him as a maverick in an industry which prides itself on being liberal.

Milius is widely regarded as the best writer of the so-called "USC Mafia," a tight-knit group of filmmakers which resuscitated—though some say homogenized—American cinema in the 1970s. Perhaps it's his politics that have kept him from being as prolific as his friends, who include box office champions Steven (Spielberg), George (Lucas), Francis (Coppola), and Robert (Zemeckis). But the fact is, his tastes are different; consequently, so is his commercial clout. Every Milius film has been conceived in struggle, born of grit, and tempered by the fires of Development hell. It's a grueling gauntlet but he has achieved an astonishing record in three decades.

"I'm probably going to be the last writer to have twenty-three credits," he laments. "People don't get a lot of credits any more; they get rewritten so much. There were so many movies I shoulda done that were done by inferior people, and they can never be done again." Indeed, a comparison of his original scripts with some of the films that others made from them reveals that they were wrong and he was right. How does this happen? Says Milius, "It's Hollywood, that's how it happens."

His taste in film—his own and other people's—is decidedly classical. Raised on Ford, Hawks, Lean, and Kurosawa, shaped by filmmakers as disparate as Fellini and Delmer Daves, Milius favors history books over comic books, character over special effects, and heroes with roots in reality, not stardust. His reputation as a historian infuses his scripts with a keen sense of time, place, and customs, and when they describe complex military maneuvers and procedures (such as in *The Greatest Raid of All* or *Rough Riders*), they are both vivid and forthright. If there is a burr under his saddle, it is that so much of what he writes winds up being directed (often badly) by "hipper" people. Nevertheless, Milius struggles forward with his own projects with the confidence of a battle-hardened general who knows how to win the war if only those damned politicians would let him. The fact that he has succeeded so often is a testament to his skills.

Milius is a captivating raconteur. A conversation with him is like sitting around a campfire, and—unusual for Hollywood—his tales are rarely about himself, but limn the drama of history. When he intones, "You know, it's interesting...," it invariably is. He insists that he honed this ability as a surfer, yet the precision of his language exceeds the argot of those who hang ten. Milius's stories reflect his own deeply held ethic embracing the values of tradition, adventure, spiritualism, honor, and an intense loyalty to friends. For an interviewer, not having to untangle spoken words is a blessing. Milius is one of only five people I have met who has this mouth-to-page facility.

So this is probably a good place to disclose that John and I have known each other for something like 45 years. Though I had first heard of him from George Hamilton who touted him as the "truly talented young writer" who had just written his film, *Evel Knievel* (1971) we only met after he made his directorial debut with *Dillinger* (1973). I discovered him to be refreshingly honest and happily indifferent that his political conservatism placed him at odds with most of his peers. This, plus his fondness for macho themes, not surprisingly made him a frequent critics' target. Pauline Kael, the former *New Yorker* reviewer, once wrote that if there were to be any animals shot during the making of a Milius film, Milius himself got to do it. Other legends hold that his contracts demand that every producer give him a new gun, that he almost killed John Huston, and that he once actually refused to accept money for a writing assignment (although he did accept tribute of a Chevy Suburban filled with Cuban cigars). Similarly, he was happy to write a new opening scene for the 1983 Chuck Norris film, *Lone Wolf McQuade*, whose director, Steve Carver, was his frequent shooting partner. Further, I was paying him a visit one Friday afternoon when he was finalizing plans to go trap shooting over the weekend with two people I'd never thought of as having an interest in guns: Steven Spielberg and Jeffrey Katzenberg. The idea of the man who opposed guns so much that he used CGI to replace them with walkie-talkies in *E.T.* confused me. But, then, in Hollywood, it's the idea, not the ideology.

He once told (baited?) me that I was the only liberal film critic he liked; whether this says more about him or me, we never decided. The subject came up over *Red Dawn* (1984). He had just come from a tour of the Pentagon conducted by General Alexander Haig, Ronald Reagan's one-time Chief of Staff. John excitedly described the experience: "they have separate floors for each branch of the services, they have these neat uniforms and grand oil paintings hanging everywhere, and you have to get around in a golf cart..." Listening to his enthusiasm, I soon realized that he was describing the building more than the institution. Finally, pausing to light a cigar, he asked, "You ever been to the Pentagon, Nat?"

"Well," I offered nostalgically, "I demonstrated outside of it a couple of times."

John raised his eyebrow, puffed the cigar thoughtfully, and said, "We have more in common than you like to think, and it bugs the shit out of you."

Like Ford, Hawks, and other filmmakers he admires, Milius' works address heroes, leadership, loyalty, duty, friendship, professionalism, and the difficulty maintaining those ideals in an amoral and confusing world. In his lexicon the worst thing to be is *stupid*, and the worst sin is to be dishonorable. Although he privately chafes at his public image as a gun-toting, Liberal-baiting provocateur, he allows himself to be painted as such, at times even holding the brush. He plays the Hollywood game like a pro, yet sticks to his own rules; he is a romantic filmmaker who avoids love scenes; his movies contain violence, yet no death in them is without meaning. Most frustrating, his best-known writing has been in films that other people wound up directing, sometimes without giving him credit.

No one is more aware of his paradoxes than Milius himself. For example, the day after *Farewell to the King* opened (disappointingly) in 1989, I dropped by his house where he and his then-wife overlooked one of Los Angeles's most picturesque canyons. As we walked through the living room we were trailed by an attentive terrier that was tap-dancing behind us on the tile floor. John waited for the tiny thing to catch up, and then gazed down at it in disgust.

"That's Posie," he grunted. "A guy like me, you'd figure I'd have a dog named *Fang*."

John Milius, the youngest of three children (Bill and Betty are older siblings), was born on April 11, 1944 to Elizabeth Roe and William Styx Milius of St. Louis, Missouri. The elder Milius was 56 at the time, and the vast age difference kept him, by his son's admission, "a distant figure, sort of a Churchillian, statesman-like figure." When John was seven, his father retired, sold the family shoe manufacturing business, and moved everybody to Southern California, joining the Golden State's postwar population boom.

By the age of 14, John had become both an avid surfer and a juvenile delinquent, two pursuits that went hand-in-hand "in the old days," as he would later call them in his autobiographical *Big Wednesday* (1978). He acquired the nickname "Viking

Man" for his flamboyance, and began honing his narrative skills in the story-swapping sessions that the beach community shared when the tide was out.

"Surfers in those days were more literate than the image of surfers today," he explains wistfully. "You must remember that surfers then had a great beatnik tradition. The first time that the great waves of Waimeia Bay were ridden, Mickey Muñoz quoted the St. Crispen's Day speech to the other surfers before they rode." But such traditions were invisible to parents, and John's shipped him to the Lowell Whiteman School in the mountains of Steamboat Springs, Colorado for eleventh and twelfth grade. By the time he returned to California he was developing into a first-rate raconteur and a recidivist surfer. Undecided whether to become an artist or a historian, he spent a summer in Hawaii where, on a day too rainy to surf, he wandered into a Kurosawa film festival. That did it. Returning home, he enrolled in the then-undergraduate Cinema School of the University of Southern California at a time when the term *student filmmaker* wasn't even a gleam in Eastman Kodak's yellow eye. By the time he got out in 1968, that changed; soon after, so would Hollywood.

USC, however, offered no automatic entree to Hollywood. Indeed, the film industry was largely a closed shop when Milius and his generation (George Lucas, Steven Spielberg, Martin Scorsese, Brian DePalma, Randal Kleiser, etc.) sought access. What blew the doors open was a combination of fresh talent and the fact that the old-line studios didn't have a clue what the burgeoning youth market wanted to see, and a plummeting box office to prove it. Thus, when Milius *et al* arrived, the time was as right as it was for Patton at the close of World War II when he urged America to invade Russia. Unlike the Third Army, however, the "USC Mafia" struck hard against the major studios, finding allies (and eager exploitation) in the likes of independent producers such as Roger Corman, Samuel Z. Arkoff, Joe Solomon, and Larry Gordon. With the collusion of Francis Coppola, who had made inroads as the first film school graduate to land a studio career, the movie brats changed the shape of film, both artistically and commercially. By the time that the blockbuster *Jaws* (Steven Spielberg, 1975) consigned all previous grosses to Davy Jones's Locker, it could be said that the New Hollywood had its finger firmly up the pulse of the public. And John Milius was its most celebrated writer.

At the time of these interviews, Milius was married to actress Elan Oberon, who was his third wife. His first marriage was to Renee Fabri, with whom he has two sons, Ethan (named after John Wayne's character in *The Searchers*) and Marcus; and his second was to Celia Kaye, with whom he has a daughter, Amanda.

I believe what follows to be the most revealing and unguarded that John has ever been.

*   *   *

NOTE: *For coherence and continuity, these interviews—some of which took place over nearly fifty years—have been edited into a chronology that reflects Milius's life, career, and philosophy.*

Growing Up American

Nat Segaloff: Before you, who was the storyteller in your family?

John Milius: My father would read or tell me stories; I remember he read James Fenimore Cooper to me. But one of the very first stories that he ever read me which told me something about him was the Rough Riders. He was quite taken; they were his heroes. He went to World War One and, when he grew up—he was Harvard, Class of 1910—he would go up to Colorado and work summers. My father was a lot older; he didn't sire me till he was 56. So my father, even though I was somewhat close to him, was a distant, sort of Churchillian, statesman-like figure. He was a pretty good woodsman, so there was a tradition in our family to do that. I remember that I was sent to various camps, and they were pretty rough, not like the usual summer camps that kids go to. The best of them was the Cottonwood Gulch Foundation, which still exists, and my kids have gone there. That was in New Mexico where you lived with the Zuni Indians and learned woodcraft. It was a kind of early Outward Bound school.

You were born April 11, 1944 in St. Louis, Missouri. Your father was a shoe manufacturer who retired and moved the family to California. Why?

He thought it would be nicer out here for the kids to grow up.

And yet he sent you to Steamboat Springs, Colorado for secondary school.

That's because I was a bad kid. By the time I was a teenager I was well into surfing and was a juvenile delinquent.

The two of them didn't go hand in hand in those days?

Yeah, most surfers were rebellious youths.

You moved out when you were seven and didn't get into surfing until you were, what, fourteen?

Eleven or twelve.

Before your bar mitzvah?

I was never bar mitzvah. We didn't have a religious family.

You told me once that you were born Jewish but that you were a practicing pagan.

Yeah, but I've become Jewish as I've grown older. It's in the blood; I can't help it. I've given up Thor. I've given up any form of idolatry.

When did your asthma develop?

I had it pretty much from when I was a kid. Most of my life.

Is that what kept you out of the military?

Yeah. I thought it would keep me out of *everything* at various times.

You were hospitalized for it?

Oh, I'd have to go in occasionally to get injections and stuff. I hated all the medicine I had to take.

I notice you're smoking a cigar.

Cigars never affected my asthma, even when I was young.

Do you take it all the way in?

Oh, heavens no! They actually calm me down to some degree. They sort of work as an anti-allergen. Asthma is brought on by extreme allergies. And I'm allergic to everything.

It would be romantic to say that you couldn't go out and play with the other kids, so you stayed inside and read books. But what did turn you on to great literature?

Oh, I went out and played all the time. I was never a particularly avid reader [but] I'd find books that were interesting to me. I was absolutely fascinated by aviation when I was young. Airplanes and the old west. Just the greatest thing in the world was to see a Corsair fly over, or a Thunderbolt or B-29 or B-17 fly over near the base.

You've said that when your father took you to see the U.S.S. Princeton in San Diego it was like going back into the womb.

There was a relative who was an Ensign serving aboard the Princeton going away to Vietnam.

There's an irony that the kid who didn't get into the Army has turned into one of our greatest filmmakers of military history.

Probably trying to make up for it. I really would have liked a military career. I work for the Army right now and I've done other things for it, so, you know, I do it my own way.

You went to the Whiteman School in Colorado because you were a rebellious youth. What turned you around there?

The mountains. The wilds of Colorado. The mountains of Colorado were like throwing B'rer Rabbit in the briar patch. Plus life was simpler and different then. For example, we were allowed to go hunting. We were allowed to check out our rifles from the closet in the school and get up in the morning and go hunting before we went in to school. You can't imagine kids doing that today in school anywhere. Any secondary school where you say you're going elk hunting, or where you say you're going to take a horse on Saturday and go up to the mountains and spend Saturday night with myself and my rifle and ammunition and a horse and some food. You can't imagine any group of adults allowing that! [Today] there'd be a million insurance things, problems. Life was a different then. We were encouraged to learn woodsmanship, how to survive in the wilds, we were encouraged to learn various sciences, bird watching, geology —

Survival sciences?

Yeah, but also things that we were fascinated with that were happening out there. We were encouraged to become naturalists. One of my teachers—Wayne Kakela—went to Dartmouth, grew up a tough, burly character, wonderful guy, very intelligent, wonderfully well-read, something of a beatnik. Before he'd become a teacher there, he'd toured the world on a motorcycle. He was a great fan of Hemingway and Faulkner. He loved great literature, and he was a great naturalist, too. We learned how to do all kinds of things—a little taxidermy, build things. One day in the afternoon we built a whole sauna, and we'd go in the sauna, and we'd get out of the sauna and go roll in the snow and a stream there. Of course, we were always trying to get the girls into the sauna!

Were you also writing then?

All of a sudden, one day, I learned how to write. Until that day, English class consisted of diagramming sentences, and I failed that miserably. I have never been able to diagram sentences; to this day I don't know the difference between an adjective and an adverb. And I didn't need to know; when it came down to writing, when I was maybe 16 or 17 years old, I could imitate any style there was. I could write a report in "Hemingway." I could write a report in "Conrad." I could write a report in "Technical Manual." I could write a report in "Kerouac."

Were you a good oral storyteller at that point?

I think I was learning. I think that comes from being a surfer. Surfers in those days were more literate than the image the surfers have today. You must remember that surfers had a great beatnik tradition. The first time that the great waives of Waimeia Bay were ridden, Mickey Muñoz quoted the St. Crispen's Day speech from *Henry V* to the other surfers before they rode. There was a different attitude about surfers.

Were you an iconoclast?

I was sort of the black sheep of the family. I was the bad kid, a decent athlete—probably a better athlete than I give myself credit for. My brother was a good football player. I probably would have been a good football player if he hadn't been a good football player. I was not a very good baseball player, though I remember, after school, once getting great pleasure from practicing double-plays. Working as a team. But I was always an outcast.

What sort of trouble did you get into?

Oh, not that much, you know, running around with a gang of kids, all very innocent: making too much noise, wising off to the cops, a few fist fights. It's all pretty innocent compared to today. Getting drunk. The good part about getting drunk lasted fifteen minutes, and then I'd get the whirlies and throw up. So by the time I was 18 I'd gone through whatever drinking I was gonna do, and never drank again. I experimented with drugs like everybody else in my generation, but, like liquor, I never saw the good side of it.

Was your car, when you were a teenager, really called the Belch Fire?

Yeah.

Guys name two things they have, and one of 'em's their car. Three, since you also named your surfboards.

I was very poetic. One of the early ones was Odin's Arrow. I was into Vikings. Then when I got to be a good surfer, I had an entire board painted red-orange, including the fins, red-orange, so they were Big Orange the Fourth and Big Orange the Tenth and Big Orange the Sixteenth and all that. Then gradually they became named after German battleships: Bismarck, Sharnhorst, Turpitz, Admiral Graf Spee... I don't know why German battleships; somehow a surf board named after a German battleship fits, rather than one called the Missouri or the Iowa or something.

You also had your own nickname, didn't you?

"Viking Man." First Viking Man, but my real name as I was growing up, in the surfing community, was The Yeti. I've always been The Yeti because I went away to school in Colorado and when I came back I was the Abominable Snowman.

Who first told you that you were a writer?

There was a good writing teacher at Whiteman, Doug Lawdor, and he encouraged me, as Wayne Kakela encouraged me. There were a number of teachers there, some of whom didn't like me at all, but they all told me that I had a gift for writing. And I knew it. I knew I could get away with a lot.

How were you at rewriting, though?

Oh, I didn't ever rewrite much. I'd get passing grades anyway, because, even though I knew nothing about the subject, I could write a pretty brilliant report.

Was Wayne Kakela your role model?

One of 'em. Growing up, I took role models out of life and literature like everybody does. John Wayne had an enormous effect on me, on everybody in my generation, and especially certain characters: Ethan Edwards or Tom Dunston, Sgt. Stryker—he was very flawed. And then another character like Gary Cooper or Bob Mitchum. But I think my favorite character in the movies was Lee Marvin. I never had a chance to work with him, but I got to know him; he was a real character. But then I had a lot of real characters I admired and learned about. I was fascinated, like other kids, by Roy Rogers and Hopalong Cassidy. Hoppy was really important. He was a little bit darker than the others—a tough, ruthless character. But there were real-life heroes, too. One of the first that I read about was Chuck Yaeger. I was aware of Chuck Yaeger from the early 50s. And Bill Bridgeman, another test pilot. I read books about them. They were the coolest of the cool. And they were *pilots*!

When you finally met Yaeger —

He was as good as I expected. A wonderful man.

The USC Film Mafia

Nat Segaloff: It's an understatement to say that you and your USC classmates changed film forever, but what was it like while you were actually there?

John Milius: There were only five undergraduate students when I went to USC: me, George Lucas, Basil Pouledoris, Randal Kleiser, and Don Glut.[1]

Film students are usually the most rebellious people on campus.

We were totally rebellious. Cinema school was situated between the school and the girls' dorm, so all these beautiful girls would go by, and we had a little berm in front of the Cinema school and we would sit on the berm and attempt to make conversation and try to get to know the girls. And, of course, we were a dismal failure. Those girls wanted nothing to do with us. We were not even geeks, we were trolls—*film* trolls!

Film wasn't cool yet.

No, it wasn't cool at all. I got my share of girls at the beach, but I like to think about all those beautiful girls going by George Lucas. He's probably never gotten over that. I remember, when I was in high school, that that was the ugliest part of life: the high

---

[1] A head count of graduate students as well as undergraduates for the years 1965-70 would add Hal Barwood, Chuck Braverman, John Carpenter, Bill Coutourie, Robert Dalva, Bob Gale, Willard Huyck, Howard Kazanjian, Walter Murch, Dan O'Bannon, Matthew Robbins, David S. Ward, and Robert Zemeckis.

school shenanigans, the popularity and all the crap that goes on. I couldn't wait to get out of high school where, of course, I was a flagrant outsider and not particularly well-accepted. Now, however, I find myself, at age 56, living in a world that has become very much like the world that I was in when I was 16 and in high school. Our whole world, our whole culture, is like a giant high school dance. But particularly Hollywood.

Did USC really create the John Milius Violence Award and give it to you one year?

I think that was the award they gave to someone else; it was named after me. They gave a plastic .38 as the John Milius Violence Award, like the Jean Hersholt Humanitarian Award.

Your 480 (thesis film) was an animation: Marcello, I'm So Bored.[2] It has a kind of Chagall-esque quality

It just fit the times and the project. I wanted to do something that was very colorful. It was dealing with hipness and fashion and that kind of stuff.

Why didn't you stay in animation?

It was the only job offer I got when I got out of school, but I couldn't see myself sitting there drawing cel after cel.

Was the industry scouting people?

They didn't scout anybody then. I was lucky to get something to do. I suppose I would have taken that job in animation if I hadn't gotten the job writing.

---

2   The film is a pastiche of captured conversations with posterized images of biker bars, people talking, and the recurring motif of a street sweeper. At the end (photographed in negative), a man and a woman drive up in a convertible. Milius plays the man. The film eventually won the National Student Film Festival award.

You also worked on other student films, too, like Glut, The Emperor, Baby Blue and Viking Women Don't Care. Were you recognized for your talents?

I was recognized, probably, as the only guy who really wanted to be a writer. But I used to joke that they all wanted to be artists. And they said, "What do you want to be?" And I said, "I want to be a big mogul and ride around in the big car." And, of course, *they* became the moguls.

Was film seen as a way to make money?

Nobody knew how to make their next penny. People at that time just wanted to do this. They didn't care whether they got very much money. Of course, I got a tremendous amount of money right away early in my career: I got a hundred thousand dollars. A hundred thousand dollars to a young surfer with no responsibilities—I was rich as a rajah!

How did you pay your way through school?

My father made a deal with me. I had different jobs, and he'd give me a dollar for every dollar I earned.

Were you doing Glut and Marcello, I'm So Bored at the same time?

Marcello took a long time to do; animation is very labor-intensive. My partner on it, John Strawbridge,[3] was a sort of genius. He designed an entire animation stand to shoot it on, and I think he actually sold the design to Hanna-Barbera.

What was the first feature script you wrote?

---

3 John Strawbridge became a leading casting associate in films and TV.

I suppose the first script I ever completed was a script there called *Los Gringos*. I think I wrote some 3x5 cards and tried to do an outline.

Was it developed with a faculty advisor?

Irwin Blacker[4] taught me how to write as a screenwriter. He was the writing teacher at USC and everyone was afraid of him and afraid of taking his course because he was very strict. But he would tell stories of Hollywood. Most of the professors had not been out in the professional world; they did documentaries and artsy films. There was something very attractive to me about Hollywood, where you could have your throat cut at any minute, where you could get rich, where you could sleep with beautiful women, and be pushed into obscurity in a half of a millisecond. *That* was the real world.

The film generation was known for taking a Beaulieu or an Éclair out in the field and just shooting. What led you into the discipline of writing?

No one else wanted to be a writer. They were all doing just what you said: putting pieces of film together. If you look at a film like *The Emperor*,[5] it was clearly made from putting pieces together. Very well done, but clearly not a *written* film. I became a writer because I wanted to be a story teller and had stories I wanted to tell.

Having turned down a job offer to do animation, how did you find yourself at American International Pictures working for producer Larry Gordon? This would have been around 1967.

---

4 Author and screenwriting teacher who mentored many USC cinema students.
5 George Lucas' documentary profiles flamboyant Los Angeles radio personality Bob "The Emperor" Hudson.

Somehow [USC classmate] Willard Huyck got a job in the story department at AIP[6] and they needed another smart-ass young college kid. It was another summer being a lifeguard or working in a gas station or doing that, so I got this job and went to work. Jim Nicholson had just separated from the company from Sam Arkoff. We would read scripts and talk to Larry and be his whipping boys. We lasted two weeks.

Describe for me, if you would, please, Mr. Milius, the circumstances of your departure.

I was fired for insubordination and Willard was fired for surliness. But we were re-hired on Monday and told to go write a script which was called *The Devil's 8*. We were told we had two weeks, and we wrote it in ten days.

This was AIP's knockoff of The Dirty Dozen (Robert Aldrich, 1967).

Yes. We wrote it in a rented apartment below the Sunset Strip. A lot of crime. I remember that our apartment—maybe someone had lent it to Willard—had a stuffed leopard in it, and I was allergic to leopard, as I was allergic to cats, having my allergies and asthma, so I had to sit out on the balcony. There was a screen door and I would yell in stuff to him and he would type it.

Were you proud of the script?

I don't think we were proud of ourselves. I don't think we ever thought it was our best work. It was pretty good; it was funny. It's a moonshine ring; a lot of noise but not very good action.

Did you go to the set?

---

6   AIP was a feisty independent company formed in 1952 by James H. Nicholson and Samuel Z. Arkoff. Arkoff (with Richard Trubo) wrote a splendid reminiscence called *Flying Through Hollywood By the Seat of My Pants* (NY: Carol Publishing Group,

Hell, no.

Even at low-budget AIP the writer was barred?

Sure, sure. And it didn't take them very long to make it. It was called *The Devil's 8* because they didn't have enough money for a full dozen.

On the strength of that, did you get an agent?

On the strength of that I probably wouldn't have gotten *anything*. I had some ideas and treatments and sent them to various agencies. I kept the letters of rejection. They said things like, "We only deal with sophisticated, well-dressed and well-washed people." Meaning that my story wasn't about sophisticated, well-dressed and well-washed people—and probably that *I* wasn't a particularly well-dressed and well-washed person. I was living in a bomb shelter underneath a house in Beverly Glen Canyon, and across the street there was a successful literary agent. I went over and talked to him and he said, "I've been watching you through this past year. How do you ever expect to be a writer? You have no discipline! All you live for is being a surfer and having pleasure and bringing these girls back to your place. That's all I ever see you with!" And he went on and on about all the girls I'd been bringing back; he'd been watching me from across the street! Needless to say, he didn't represent me.

Did The Devil's 8 *launch your career?*

You gotta understand, when you got something done at AIP, especially something like *The Devil's 8*, that wasn't necessarily a boon to anything. Plus you must remember that writers in those days—as opposed to today, where there are a lot of very successful writers who have no credits and there are a lot of writers with one or two credits—in those days, writers had twenty or thirty credits. I'm the last writer like that in the business. I'm the last writer who has twenty-three credits. There aren't going to be any more writers like that; people don't get a lot of credits any more. They get rewritten so much now that very few people get a lot of credits.[7]

What agent finally represented you?

I don't remember their names, to tell you the truth, but they had very nice offices in Beverly Hills, and they sent me out on TV assignments where I was rejected and scolded by the TV executives. I'd come up with a great story, but the TV executives would say, "You're just making that up! You're making it up right now! You're not dealing with the structure of our series!" It was pretty horrible. The next assignment I got, right after AIP, was to write a thing called *The Texans* for Al [Albert S.] Ruddy. He was making *Little Fauss and Big Halsey* (Sidney J. Furie, 1970) at the time. I'd written another screenplay after *Los Gringos* called *Last Resort*, and won the National Student Film Festival [for *Marcello*], and then my friends George Lucas and Marty Scorsese and I were all featured in *Time* magazine—all the ugly, punk kids. Mike Medavoy, who was working in the mail room of CMA (Creative Management Associates), said he would represent us all. That was in 1968. Needless to say, he was a good agent and did well.[8] And then I did a script called *Truck Driver* which was a pretty good story, though it never got made. I traveled around the country with truck drivers, going to all the truck driving hangouts, watching them get into fights and fall in love with whores. It was a pretty colorful group. The

---

7 This is a reference to the current practice of hiring additional writers to rewrite, doctor, or polish scripts, or bringing in people to add "action" or "character" or "jokes"—basically because a producer or film company executive doesn't really know what he wants except to cover his ass—and leave the WGA to sort out the screen credits through arbitration. It also addresses the ongoing quandary of why someone would like a script enough to buy it, and then go about ruining it with changes.

8 A key player in the creation of the "New Hollywood," Medavoy became production chief of United Artists, left to co-found Orion Pictures, and later formed his own company, Phoenix Pictures.

script wasn't that good because it drifted from the truck drivers into having a little more social commentary. But the basic premise was good. I wrote that for Levy-Gardler-Laven, for Arnold Laven, a very nice man. Somehow or other I just knew I was gonna keep doing stuff, that Medavoy would bring me another job. And I followed that with *Jeremiah Johnson*.

Writing for Others to Direct

Nat Segaloff: Jeremiah Johnson has a complicated history. You had written the script, and then it was pulled away from you and given to Edward Anhalt, then you were brought back in.

John Milius: Twice! I got very little money to write it. I got $5,000 to write it but by the time I was through I had made $80,000. That's how many times they hired, fired, and re-hired me.

The original story is about a guy who kills 247 Crow Indians.[9]

I don't remember how many, but he killed a lot of Crow and he ate their livers. He lived till about 90-something so they couldn't have been that bad, those Crow livers. When Warner Bros. bought it, Sydney Pollack was not the director, nor was Robert Redford the star. The first considered star was going to be Clint Eastwood, and the director was to be Sam Peckinpah. Sam was working on the movie and I was really looking forward to doing it with Sam; he was one of my heroes. But he didn't last very long; he went and had a meeting with Eastwood, and ten minutes after the meeting, he was gone. I was working on another Warner Bros. picture at the time, *Dirty Harry*, which was going to star Frank Sinatra. Frank Sinatra quit, so they

---

9   When a Cavalry officer prevails on mountain man Jeremiah Johnson to lead him through a sacred Crow burial site, the Crow retaliate by killing Johnson's adopted wife and son. Johnson then goes on a rampage killing Crow Indians until he and the tribe reach, at best, a respectful stand-off.

moved Clint Eastwood into *Dirty Harry* and took him off *Crow Killer*, which became *Jeremiah Johnson*. They thought they had a hot script and they could get anybody, so they wanted Redford, who was the hottest thing in Hollywood at the time—the Brad Pitt or the Leonardo DiCaprio of his day.

Was the character changed because it would have hurt Robert Redford's image to have him go around killing 247 Crow Indians?

It was softened quite a bit, but, still, remember, he *was* a man named "Liver-Eating Johnson."

Edward Anhalt told William Froug (in The Screenwriter Looks at Screenwriting, NY: MacMillan, 1972) that "John Milius, the original writer, was committed to one kind of story and the producers weren't. I thought his script was brilliant, but I don't know how many people would have paid to see it." My question is—and we'll keep getting into this—why did they buy the script if they didn't want to make the movie?

That's the question that is constantly asked in Hollywood. There is no answer.

The material and characters are so rich, yet the dialogue is minimalist.

Even though the scenes were reconstructed, I had to do all the dialogue eventually in the film, every line, because no one else could do the dialogue. They brought in Edward Anhalt, they brought in David Rayfiel, who is on every Sydney Pollack film, and a good writer, but nobody could get the mountain men dialogue. I always wanted them to say very little. The point of being a mountain man is that he's out there alone and he doesn't see anybody or talk to anybody, and when he does see somebody, the guy more than likely wants to kill him. Mountain men talked colorfully. I got the idiom from Carl Sandburg. [For example] Johnson comes up to a trapper named Del Gue, played by Stefan Gierash, who's buried up to his neck in the sand. First of all, he says, "How're you doin'?" And because he says, "How're you doin'?" Del Gue says, "Oh, I'm doin' fine, I got a fine horse buried under me." Later he says, talking about scalps, "Mother Gue never raised such a foolish child" or "you have stolen these pelts and die you must." That's not normal language. You know where I got a lot of that from? The book *True Grit* by Charles Portis, who wrote the book without contractions, so that people say, "I *will* do that" and not "I'll do that."

JOHNSON
Where is it that I could find bear, beaver and other critters worth cash money when skinned?

MAN
Ride due west as the sun sets. Turn left at the Rocky Mountains.

Another example is when Johnson finds a man frozen in the ice, but he's left a note: "I, Hatchet Jack, being of sound mind and broke legs do hereby giveth my bear rifle to whatever finds it. Lord hope it be a white man. My horse run off. I do not press the loss of the animal, but he had a forty dollar saddle. Anyway, I am dead." I think you can truthfully say, although other movies of mine had been made by then, and *Evel Knievel* is full of good stuff, too, that *Jeremiah Johnson* is where I was getting up to speed.

We're not supposed to know Johnson's past, although the man singing the ballad at the beginning says, "...bettin' on forgettin' all the trouble that he knew." We also know, from the remnants of his uniform, that he was in the army.

The Mexican Wars. He was like a Vietnam vet. He's gone off to an unpopular war, he's seen war, he doesn't like what Man has done and he wants to go to the purity of the high, tall hills where there is very few people "and there ain't no asylums for the crazy ones."

What was it like getting the call that said, "Um, er, John, we can't quite lick this dialogue, would you come back...?"

I don't really remember; they just called up. Sydney Pollack always looked at me like I was crazy or was going to do something horrible or attack everybody or start gnawing on human flesh.

Johnson brings trouble upon himself when he breaks the Crow rules and leads the Army though their sacred burial ground. Yet since he transgressed first, what gives him the moral right to go tracking down Crow?

It doesn't matter. Once the thing is set in motion you have to go with it. There is no right and wrong. The mountains decide the right and wrong. It is, in fact, important that he does transgress first, that he does go through the burial ground, because sooner or later he's going to be set against, and there is going to be a feud. The feud will go on forever, and it makes both of them bigger and makes them live forever and also kills them. And these are the way all feuds are, the way the Hatfields and the McCoys are, the Capulets and the Monatgues, and the feuds in Borneo among the Dayaks. When I was making *Farewell to the King* in Borneo I'd ask the Dayaks, "What started this feud?" and they'd say, "It doesn't matter. The feud has been here since the time of God."

How would you yourself have made Jeremiah Johnson if you'd directed it?

Much more ferocious. Nobody's ever faced the ferocity of the mountain men. There have been no movies where they dealt with these guys honestly. They always like to make them colorful old hermits, they like them to be early ecologists who live out there worried about the spoilage of cleaning beavers upstream, and what's gonna happen when the covered wagons come in. Mountain men are always portrayed by most people as at the end of their time: "The west was a wonderful place! This was a shinin' place! But it ain't no more. Now there are wagons goin' to Oregon and it's all over..." The beauty of the Mountain Men was the beginning of their time, when they were the first—like Jedediah Smith who had a craving to find out what was over the next mountain. The era of exploration. There's a wonderful painting of Frederic Remington's called "The Unknown Explorers"—two mountain men and these huge, treed cliffs at twilight and you get the sense that these are the first white men there, and it's absolutely pure. That's what it was to be a mountain man, and why they were willing to lead the violent life and be as ferocious as the Indian. That must have been marvelous. But I liked the film a great deal, and I liked Sydney's vision. I give him full credit for that.

Now we come to Dirty Harry. You are not credited, but you and Terry Malick wrote an early draft of the screenplay along with H.J. [Harry Julian] Fink. The original title of Dirty Harry was Dead Right —

— naw, it was always *Dirty Harry* —

— and that it was changed when Frank Sinatra was attached to it, and Irvin Kershner was set to direct. At what point did Don Siegel come in?

He came in an hour after Irvin Kershner left. We went to Palm Springs for our second meeting with Frank Sinatra where we were driven by circuitous route to his compound by one of his thugs. We had a lunch of finger sandwiches, where they cut off the crusts, very nicely done. He had asked me the first time about "the gat." I said, "What?" and he said, "You know, the gun. Do you have one of those big guns?" I said, "Yeah, I'll bring one next time." Well, I don't think he thought this kid was gonna bring a gun, a gat. So on the second meeting he asked me about "the gat" and I opened my brief case and whipped out my four-inch model 29. And he said, "Jilly [his bodyguard], look! Lookit that gun! Lookit that gat! He comes in here with a gat that big and you don't even know it!" Needless to say, I think Jilly got in a lot of trouble for that. But Frank picked up the "gat" and looked at it. He'd had his hand operated on for something or other and he couldn't play the piano very well, but he picked up the gun and said the line that's in the script, "Ooh, it's a big one!" And he said, "too big!" and put the gun back in my brief case. We went back to Los Angeles from Palm Springs and by the time we got here they said that he had decided he didn't want to be in the movie business any more. I thought that somehow I had driven Frank Sinatra from the movie business with my .44 magnum. Anyway, to show how they operated in those days, they didn't change the art department, they didn't change the schedule, they didn't change the release date, they didn't change anything. They simply went and told Kershner that they were going to do it with somebody else, most likely Burt Lancaster or Eastwood, and they decided on Clint Eastwood because he was the youngest and they figured they could do more stuff with him. Since Clint Eastwood had worked with Don Siegel on other movie,[10] it took them another hour to call Don Siegel. So nobody even knew that Frank Sinatra had quit or that the director had been replaced; it wasn't even a hiccup. Today if that happened, they'd just cancel the movie.

---

10 *Coogan's Bluff, Two Mules for Sister Sarah* and *The Beguiled.*

Your script starts quite differently from the finished film, which begins with Scorpio on a roof top shooting a girl in her swimming pool.

Mine started with Harry ranting at the audience as if they were young cops being trained, standing in front of pictures of dead cops, shooting melons and stuff with different weapons. Did you like that scene?

Yes, I did, but it changes Harry's character. It makes him seem crazy.

I didn't think he was crazy, but Clint Eastwood said—and he's right—"I don't do those words. George Scott does those words. I'm good at grunting and squinting and shooting people, mostly squinting. I don't do words, I do squinting." Clint Eastwood was very clear on what he could and couldn't do, and molded the character pretty much the way he wanted to. That script was where I really learned a lot of tricks. I learned how to cut from one thing to another, how to cut pieces off of the scene—wonderful tricks like where Scorpio's making demands: "I want a bus, I want money—" and cut to the bus. He says he's going to do something, and then you cut to what he's doing, getting onto a bus full of children.

Did you and Terry Malick work together on it?

No. They brought Terry Malick in after I left to do *Judge Roy Bean*.

The "I know what you're thinkin'" speech is yours.[11]

---

11   For the record, Harry says to the felled bank robber, "I know what you're thinkin': 'Did he fire six shots or only five?' Well, to tell you the truth, in all this excitement I kinda lost track myself. But being as this is a .44 Magnum, the most powerful hand gun in the world, and would blow your head clean off, you've got to ask yourself one question, 'Do I feel lucky?' Well, do you, punk?"

Yeah.

I hate to tell you this, but in the shootout at beginning of the film, he does fire only five shots, so he should have one left to shoot the robber.[12]

Are you sure?

What's interesting is that the theme of vigilantism which drew so much criticism in Dirty Harry *becomes the very essence of* Magnum Force.

Magnum Force is the flip side of Dirty Harry; in other words, if you can go beyond the law, how far can you go? To me, the idea of those two films is that one brings up the moral question that the other brings up. It's not just a sequel. A sequel in Hollywood is just more of the same; there's no intelligence to these things. Sequels to movies today have no right to be movies at all, it's just "give us more of the same." When they were doing the sequel to Jaws, I remember that they said, "We're gonna have a lot more pretty girls eaten by sharks, and maybe some more people and young kids and puppies in jeopardy." More shark, more people eaten, more situations where people are menaced by sharks! That's what they thought made the first movie go. That's not what made the first movie go; the first movie was about pride of species. When you see the first movie there should have been a speech that says, "These sharks have been around 60 million years, we haven't been around nearly that long, but we've been around long enough that we're gonna win, because this is between Man and sharks, and we're men and we want to win." And that's what happens: in the end you blow up the shark and it feels good. There's no ecology, no tree-hugging attitude about it. The shark needs to get what he gets. It's back to the days when leopards and lions were challenging us. Which wasn't very long ago.

---

12 I admit it's a toss-up. Harry fires two shots on camera; there's a third shot off camera; and three more on camera. My conjecture is that the third shot was added in post-production when the filmmakers realized the count was off.

Dirty Harry was criticized for being fascist—

That's just because Pauline Kael liked the sound of that word. She liked to call me a fascist and called me a fascist for years. *She* was a fascist!

The Paulettes, you mean?[13]

Um-hmm.

In Reeling *(NY: Warner Books, 1976), referring to* Jeremiah Johnson, *she writes, "he had it written into his contract…that he would get to shoot the numerous animals that his script (later modified) required be slaughtered."*

I just said that if you want somebody to shoot an elk, I'd like to shoot the elk because I'd like the meat. And that's what she turned it into. Obviously, there are no animals killed on camera in that movie.

Was it really a part of your employment deal in the early days that your producer had to give you a new gun?

Yes. Because paper wasn't honorable. People were more honorable in those days.

When did this stop being part of your contract?

When the price of my screenplays went above $500,000, they said, "You can get your own Goddamn gun."
It seems to me that the other bad guys in Dirty Harry— *besides Scorpio (Andrew Robinson)—are the politicians. Not*

---

13 It has long been asserted that the esteemed New Yorker critic led a coterie of well-placed younger critics whom she placed in their jobs, and whose views she heavily influenced—some say dictated. Adherents informally call themselves "Kaelites," while those not in her thrall dismiss them as "Paulettes."

necessarily liberal or conservative, but the ones who are more concerned with their own image than with upholding the law.

I always thought the thing was just about logic. It's an unwritten law; we know who's guilty and who isn't and what has to be done. The whole idea of Dirty Harry is that he's the other side of that; he's not too far from Andy Robinson, he's just on *our* side. He's a hunter.

The "given" is that we know who the bad guy is because we see him doing it.

Harry knows who Scorpio is. *Everybody* knows who Scorpio is. Everybody *knows* Scorpio needs to be dead. That's why you have Harry.

But you have to know for sure that the miscreant is the correct person.

These are cases where it's not a question.

Were you involved in every stage of Dirty Harry or did you turn in your version and that was it?

I did my version and then I left. I wanted to stay. Clint had me do a couple of things, but then I was off on the set of *Judge Roy Bean* so I didn't even really know what was going on.

Harry's character has a very interesting arc. By the time of The Enforcer (Clint Eastwood, 1983)—which you didn't write— Sondra Locke is a woman who kills rapists and, at the end, Harry lets her get away with it. He breaks his own Javertian rules.

Well, Sondra Locke was Clint Eastwood's girlfriend then, so that might've had something to do with it.

Becoming Bloodied

Nat Segaloff: Your best written script, as a reading script, is still, I think, The Life and Times of Judge Roy Bean. *You intended making your directorial debut with it, didn't you, but then Paul Newman got involved?*

John Milius: It was sent to Lee Marvin. He and Lee Marvin were making a movie (*Pocket Money;* Stuart Rosenberg, 1972) and Lee Marvin got the script and he was reading it and he really liked it and he got drunk and he left it on his chair and went off and passed out somewhere. Newman picked it up and started reading it and took it away, and called his people in Los Angeles and said, "Buy this script, I want to do this." So they came to me and they wanted to buy the script. And I said, "Fine, I want to direct it." They said, "No, no, that's not possible." So there were two prices: one that was very cheap with me directing it, and one that kept going up and up if they wanted it without me, and they finally paid the price without me. It was considerably mutilated by the time it was made. John Huston changed all kinds of things or demanded that I change it. It wasn't at all the same movie.[14]

---

14 Judge Roy Bean yearns his entire life to meet Lily Langry, but before this can happen he is killed defending his town against bad men. In Milius's script, Langry arrives by train the morning after Bean dies and is handed a letter he left behind for her. The script says, "She sat in the window, framed like a beautiful portrait. Reflected in that window, one could also see the Judge's coffin being loaded onto the train. She opened the letter and read. . .a tear rolled down her cheek—she sniffed but recomposed herself by stiffening the upper lip. She folded the letter—the train whistle blew—clouds of steam obscured her. The train left with the two of them. That is the story of how Judge Roy Bean lived and died and brought law and order to the wild land west of the Pecos River. Fade Out." In the film, years pass between Bean's death and Langtry's arrival. The emotion is dissipated, but it's still lovely.

***Yet later you hired Huston to play Secretary of State John Hay in* The Wind and the Lion.**

I like Huston, even though he completely ruined my script. But I don't think Huston ruined it as much as the whole group of them. I mean, they were just wrong. Huston certainly wasn't the right person to direct it, Newman certainly wasn't the right person to act in it. And they're all terrific people; Paul Newman's one of the nicest, most intelligent people in the world. I can't say anything against him; he just wasn't right for that movie.

Did I ever tell you about the time I almost killed John Huston?[15] We went hunting. It was around here; we went up to Elizabeth Lake, and I had this great dog then, named Jaster, and there were Joshua trees in that area. We were hunting quail and we got into a covey of quail and we were watching Jaster and shooting and Huston was saying, "This is great, this is marvelous, we're going to have a marvelous day." We're pretty far from the road, and it was really hot. So he starts coughing, and he just turns, he gets all red, and he gets under a Joshua tree and he says, "I'm gonna cash it in, kid. This is it. I'm not gonna make it, I, I can tell!"

And I said, "What can I do? What can I do?"

He says, "Go back and get some water."

It's a long way to the car in the hot sun. In those days I was in pretty good shape, so I ran all the way back, and I'm thinking, "What am I gonna do? When I get back he's gonna be dead. How am I going to explain this to the Police? To Hollywood? That I took John Huston out and killed him hunting." Of course, he killed Clark Gable the same way[16] and several other people,

---

15 Huston suffered from emphysema, which eventually killed him in 1987 (see the author's *Mr. Huston/Mr. North: Life, Death, and Making John Huston's Last Film* (Bear Manor Media, 2014).
16 Filming *The Misfits* (1960).

but he was like a father to me, and I was just horrified. So I get back, thinking, "God, I hope he's alive," and by then he's propped himself up under the tree, and he says, "Did you bring any beer?" He's still red and breathing horribly, but he's got a cigar out by then, and he says, "You didn't bring any beer!"

I said, "We don't have any beer!"

And he says, "You shoulda known, you shoulda known." Then he says, "I don't know if I can make it. I still don't know if I can make it. You better sit down. I'm gonna tell you about my first recollection of my life, since you'll probably be here for my last."

Then he tells me a story about how he was a little kid and his father, Walter, who was a worthless actor with an actor's personality, had some job in Globe, Arizona or Douglas, Arizona or some place like that. He was in charge of the volunteer fire department and, of course, since he didn't want to work and was just a ne'er-do-well, he had sold, to various restaurants and other places, all the water that was kept in the fire department's storage tanks. But he didn't tell anybody, and so when a fire breaks out in the hotel or the bar or some place like that, everybody runs out and the fire department comes, and there's no water. Well, the town burns. Soon they figured it out. So, he said, his earliest recollection of life was the town burning to the ground in the night, and an angry crowd pursuing his father with torches, tar-and-feathers, and a noose, and him bouncing in the back of a buckboard as his father high-tailed it out of town with his mother. That was his first recollection of life, and I think it's pretty damn good! Needless to say, he didn't die on me.

The real Roy Bean was more legitimate than he always claimed he was, though. He was appointed a magistrate —

Oh, he was an outlaw who claimed he was "Law West of the Pecos." There wasn't much there; he was just one of these characters running around out there.

He would change his verdict based upon how much money the accused criminal had on him.

Right, but, see, what was good was just that very fact. He was the onset of civilization. Here was this guy who was an outlaw—probably a thief and a stage robber—who set himself up as the law, and that meant that the law had come to Vinegaroon; the law had come West of the Pecos. That's how civilization arrives. It arrives in the form of someone who says, "I am the law and I'll hang whatever sonofabitch says there won't be law." And that's what the movie's about. It's about a man who brings the benefits of civilization to this place, who changes the desert into what he wants it to be, a thriving city. And, of course, it isn't a thriving city, it's a dirty little town that has all of the evils of civilization, and, ultimately, has no room for him.

As Bean says, "I know the law, having spent my entire life in its flagrant disregard." At what point was the script changed, and how did Huston lean on you to change it?

He loved to torture writers. He was a sadist. If you survived the torture well enough then he took you in as a sort of a son. I guess I survived my ordeal. I could see him ruining it. He had an assistant named Gladys Hill, and Gladys Hill looked like an old school teacher, but she was actually a smuggler who arranged everything for him. She arranged his mistresses coming and going and his various smugglers bringing in stolen pre-Columbian art. And his threat was always, "I want a change to this, kid, and if you don't, Miss Hill will change it." Of course, Miss Hill couldn't write worth a damn. Nor could he. And probably the reason he wanted the changes was that it bothered him no end that he couldn't write that well. He told me that one time.

He said, "Part of the reason I'm torturing you is you're so damn good at this, and I'll make you pay."

Huston may have been a sadist, he could also seduce the apple out of a snake's mouth.

That's right. You can say all these terrible things about him, but he was a wonderful person, a wonderful human being. I learned an enormous amount from him. My first wife claims that he was the influence that ended my marriage, but we won't get into that.

He called you "kid," which was some kind of accolade.

When he liked you a lot, he called you "Joooohhhhn." When he wanted to give you some shit, he called you "kid."

What did you learn about directing from Huston?

More than I ever learned in cinema school. Just marvelous things. He would do things wrong; he would say, "I'm gonna connect these two shots with all this complicated camera movement." And he said, "Basically, the reason I'm doing this is that it will take a long, long time to set up and I'll have time to go to the trailer and have time to look at some art or fool around with Cici,:[17] He'd confide to me, "I don't really want to be here on the set, so I'm gonna give them this enormously complex shot," a Hitchcockian *Rope* shot involving all these stunts. "But that's not the way you'd really want to do it; the way you'd really want to do it is this, this, and this." And then he used to say, "inevitably the shot that's the worst, most pretentious shot in the movie," like through a keyhole or something, "that's the shot they're always gonna show and think is so great, that's the shot the critics will always like."

---

[17] Celeste Shane, Huston's fifth wife (August 8, 1972 to July 21, 1975.) In his memoirs he called her "the crocodile"

Let's get to Evel Knievel (1971) and George Hamilton. At that time he was chiefly known as a guy who worked on his tan and dated one of President Johnson's daughters. Was your relationship a good one?

A wonderful relationship to this day. He's a wonderful guy, totally under-rated. He's a great con-man, that's what he really is. He always said, "I'll be remembered as a third-rate actor when, in fact, I'm a first-rate con man."

You weren't the first writer on the script.

I was having a fight with my wife, and George said, "I will provide you with my home in Palm Springs and a motorcycle, and you can get away from your wife for the weekend, go quail hunting, and I'll pay you $5,000—that's all I've got—to write a couple of funny lines in this script." Whatever. George was trying to find a way to lure me down there, and I wanted to get away. Well, I get down there and I read this script, and it's terrible. So I threw the script in the pool and beat on it with an oar. And, of course, now the script is waterlogged, so I wrote another one. *And he knew I was gonna do that!* He later told me he knew if I got down there with that script I'd write another one.

What's your key in the script that defines Knievel's character?

He saw himself as the new Gladiator of the new Rome, something larger than this daredevil, that he saw the whole spectacle of civilization and the absurdity of what it's turned into, and that he could see how he fit into that. A character like Liberace, a great showman, these outrageous outfits. And he would do these insane things; what's the point of driving a motorcycle over a bunch of trucks, let alone the Caesar's Palace fountain? Where does this come in? It's a stunt that doesn't even make any sense. But somehow it's wonderful because it's not just jumping through hoops of fire or over pits of snakes, it's a bunch of lined-up cars or trucks. It brings it right back down to a blue-collar, proletarian elegance to Evel Knievel.

What did Knievel himself think of the film?

He loved it. He used the opening speech in his act and followed the movie as it played around the country. He was kind of an interesting character.

Directing Dillinger

Nat Segaloff: You finally got to direct with Dillinger, which has the kind of opening scene that makes an audience pay attention: John Dillinger (Warren Oates) robs a bank and announces to the customers, "This could be one of the biggest moments in your life, don't make it your last." You drew him as a hero, but in fact he hurt people, such as when we are told by Melvin Purvis (Ben Johnson)—the G-Man who pursues him—that he killed a bank guard named O'Malley.

John Milius: Well, no; in reality there was one murder rap, and that was even unsure. That's why I picked him. Of all the gangsters, outlaws, he was the most marvelous. He said something great: "You'd do what I do if you had the nerve." But you assume that when you embark down that road, you're gonna kill somebody. That's why I had him kill O'Malley. If you live that kind of life, you're gonna have to take the consequences.

He beat up on Baby Face Nelson (Richard Dreyfuss) pretty nicely.

Baby Face Nelson was a killer. He was a rat. He deserved what he got. But Dillinger was an artist, a terrific character. His life was an example in the Depression—not that you can rob the banks and right the social ills like Bonnie and Clyde (which is totally balderdash in that movie; they had no more intention of being Robin Hood than Dillinger or Baby Face Nelson. They were always griping because they'd rob stores and get fifteen dollars and have to shoot people).

Is that why you gave the line to Pretty Boy Floyd (Steve Kanaly): "Things were all right till Bonnie & Clyde came through, and then everything went to hell."

Yeah, 'cause they were punks. Clyde was the Charlie Starkweather of his day.

Your characters behave as if they know the audience is watching, such as Homer van Meter (Harry Dean Stanton) sighing, just as the G-Men are about to gun him down, "Things have not been going well for me today."

I have a healthy sense of the absurd.

Since you were a first-timer, did the studio give you any trouble when you were shooting the film?

The dailies came in and they couldn't figure how it was going to cut together. So they sent a doom squad, this guy, out to me in Oklahoma. And I sat down and explained to him what I was doing and where the shots went. And he said, "Oh, that's what you meant!" Now, it's not a complex movie to put together. But once they did that, they never bothered me again.

How did you settle on the secret of having Dillinger and Purvis both be essentially the same character in that each is concerned about his folk image?

All that stuff you're talking about—looking after their own fame—I didn't think of it that way, really. I just thought of them as these two bigger-than-life characters who were opposed to one another, kind of like the Olympians. It's like Hector and Achilles looking over the wall at each other.

Yet it was Purvis's fame that eventually got him on J. Edgar Hoover's bad side. As you point out in the film's end credits, he committed suicide with the same gun he'd used to capture Dillinger. His son, Alston Purvis, discovered that this might have been because he couldn't get work after he left the Bureau, thanks to Hoover.

He became the Post Toasties Junior G-Man or something like that. But there wasn't an awful lot about Purvis after he captured Dillinger.

These was at least enough to get a TV movie out of it. How did Melvin Purvis: G-Man *happen?*

Larry Gordon, who had given me the opportunity to do *Dillinger*, had left AIP and said, "You owe it to me, boy, you owe it to me." So I wrote that script in five days. It was a pretty good script, but the director [Dan Curtis] was a really obnoxious character, and he was telling me what to write. I said, "I don't take orders from the likes of you" and that was that. Then he changed a lot of stuff.

Do actors struggle with period dialogue?

Sometimes if they had trouble with the lines, I'd rewrite them on the spot. I never thought of it as being literate or poetic; that's the way people spoke in the thirties—without contractions.[18]

It's a wonderful scene where Harry Dean has to get something out of the filling station that they've tried to rob, so he shoots their gumball machine.

Yeah—"I got his gumball machine." That wasn't in the script. The guy running the filling station was a character! He couldn't

---

18 The convention was also popularized by the short stories of Damon Runyon.

act at all, so I had to do something with him. I had him just say, "Yep" and the same thing over and over again and Harry Dean gets so frustrated that the guy doesn't care he's a gangster, he just shoots the gumball machine like a bully and runs away. He's reduced to that.

Did AIP tell you to put certain things in the script for commercial appeal?

No. In those days [when] they decided to make a movie, [they just did], and since I was a really hot writer in town at that moment, Larry Gordon said, "We'll let you direct the movie if you write it cheap." I would, of course, have paid *them* to direct a movie. But I wrote it cheap and directed it cheap, and, really, all the studios in those days believed in me enough that they said, "We're gonna make a movie about Dillinger, we know the script will be wonderful, go and write it." Larry Gordon had some comments—very minor sort of things, a typo on one page, or a line change. [He'd say] "I want him to be tougher here," or something like that. "I wanna see some blue pages,[19] big boy." All I did was mark all the pages that he made comments on and have them printed blue and gave 'em back to him and he liked it fine.

All right, now, we might as well settle the urban myth about John Dillinger's dick.

I could find no evidence of it, talking to the FBI then and later.

They say it comes from that news picture of his body being carried away on a gurney, covered by a sheet. His arm is at an angle beneath the sheet that looks like a huge erection, and the legend grew from there.

---

19 The convention was also popularized by the short stories of Damon Runyon.

Naw, I don't think so. But what's really kinda lovely about that—you talk about a wonderful folk tale—I love the idea that people think John Dillinger has this enormous dick because it fits into the Depression. Such a wonderful image: the man who could fight the banks, that they killed, was so potent. He was fighting the thing that had brought everyone down. He was standing up against the system. Today a criminal wouldn't have the same importance.

Robert Benton and David Newman (who wrote Bonnie and Clyde; Arthur Penn, 1967) said that one of the things that helped Bonnie and Clyde survive was that they were always careful to steal cars with V-8 engines at a time when most constabularies had squad cars with six-cylinder engines in them. Likewise, Dillinger used Thompson submachine guns.

Yes, and of course you know that Dillinger sent a letter to Henry Ford about how he only stole V-8 Fords, what a wonderful vehicle he made, and thanking him for it. They stole guns from national armories so they had B.A.R.s (Browning Automatic Rifles), Thompsons (Thompson submachine guns, or Tommy guns). But the most effective weapon was a Browning automatic.

The Wind and the Lion

Nat Segaloff: One of the things that makes the project work is that, in reality,[20] it was a man who was kidnapped, not a woman.

John Milius: I got it entirely from the Forbes[21] book. Matter of fact, the idea of making it a woman was from Forbes.

So it wasn't just a Hollywood sex change?

No. The original story, as you know, was about a man being kidnapped. But when I read the story [in the August 1959 *American Heritage* magazine] and then wanted to read more about the Raisuli, the book I got was the Forbes book. And I saw that this was the way it should be; instead of a man being kidnapped, it should be a woman, and the relationship between the two of them should be quite sensual without them ever doing anything.

Do you think Mrs. Forbes had a relationship with the Raisuli?

---

20 In 1904, Mulay Hamid El Raisuli (Sean Connery) kidnaps an American woman, Eden Pedicaris (Candace Bergen), and her children, not for money, which has no honor, but as a political ploy, causing President Theodore Roosevelt to call out the Mediterranean fleet to rescue her. In actuality, the Raisuli captured an English man named Ian Pedicaris.
21 Rosita Forbes, *El Raisuni, the Sultan of the Mountains*, England: Thornton-Butterworth, Ltd., 1924. Forbes—whose real name was Lady McGrath—was a celebrated travel writer who also influenced young filmmaker Michael Powell (q.v. Powell, Michael, see *A Life in Movies*, NY: Alfred A. Knopf, 1987).

I've always thought so. I'm almost sure. He was a captivating character. She was attractive and he would have wanted her. And he *was* the Raisuli!

The script is more brutal than the movie. For example, in the script the Raisuli's captors cut his ear off as torture, but no mention of it is made in the film.

We put some blood on his ear and you can see it when he's hanging upside down, and then he wraps himself—his turban is covering up one ear at the end—so he's lost his ear.

The Teddy Roosevelt character in the script comes off, I think, a little more callow than Brian Keith plays him. In the script, Roosevelt definitely wants to provoke a shooting war; the film makes him almost playful.

He played it pretty much the way I wrote it. There was a sort of tongue-in-cheek quality about it. Plus the idea that Imperialism wasn't a bad word then. The idea of that movie is that people think and act in a way that was correct for 1904—not correct for 1917, not correct, certainly, for 1920, and *absolutely* not correct for 1974 when the movie was made. But in 1904 Imperialism was a good thing. Everybody's doing it; we should be there first.

When Joseph, Mrs. Pedicaris' luncheon guest at the beginning of the story, questions her serving a red wine, this is, to him, the height of impropriety.

Only an American woman would do that. But it's interesting to create a window that you can look into the world that once was—that resonate to the present—but that are seen on the terms that they were seen then. They're as close as you can now get to those times. When you see *Barry Lyndon*,[22] it is beautifully done, and is uncompromising in that the scenes

---

22 Stanley Kubrick, 1974

themselves are structured as if they came from a William Thackeray novel.

When the Pedicaris boy looks at Sean Connery and says, "He has the way about him, doesn't he, mother?" that is just the expression to describe the charisma that the Raisuli must have. Were there other actors ever considered?

The only other person ever considered was Anthony Quinn, who could have been a good Raisuli, except that he was too old. Omar Sharif would have been good, but he wouldn't have been a Raisuli. It wouldn't have been the same movie; he would have been too much the ladies' man, too smooth.

Your script has a scene with Charles Foster Kane, but not the movie. Did you intend to shoot it?

Yes, and, of course, I wanted to get Orson Welles to do it. Orson Welles was making *The Other Side of the Wind*[23] in Hollywood at the time and he wanted me to be in it. Huston was in it. All of a sudden, one day, when I'm shooting in the most oppressive heat in Seville [Spain, where *The Wind and the Lion* was filmed], and I'm staying at the Alphonse XIII hotel, which they used as the Officers' Club in *Lawrence of Arabia*,[24] I come back and I'm covered in dust and sweat and there's this impeccably dressed Italian assistant director who says, "Mr. Welles is here; he'd like to see you." So I'm ushered into a Moorish back room and Welles is there with two huge fans that he's holding and he's in this giant caftan and he's covered with sweat and he's huge but he's just sitting there enjoying the evening light. He said, "I should've brought a camera; I wanted to shoot you for my movie. I had to get an actor to play you." He goes on

---

23 Welles' legendary, never-completed film about the last days of a once-great Hollywood director (played by John Huston). Many filmmakers today recall—perhaps apocryphally—how they would be summoned by Welles at all hours to "come and be in the movie" It was finally finished with Netflix backing in 2018.
24 David Lean, 1962.

and tells me how he's come there to do a sherry commercial and he's just had two ducks—*two roast ducks!* He recommends various restaurants and then he laughs and says, "I suffer from a disease—a Medieval disease—it's called *o-bes-i-ty.*" Now, can you have a better meeting with Orson Welles than that?

But he still didn't play Charles Foster Kane.

No, we had to cut that out. I think the Errors and Omissions people [studio lawyers] said, "We can't possibly put that in. We'd get sued by RKO!"

1975, when the film was released, was a year that saw the bifurcation of the American film industry. Steven Spielberg made Jaws, **and its box office success drove everybody to chase blockbusters from then on. You made** The Wind and the Lion, **which was a more traditional film. A lot has been made about how your generation of filmmakers stuck together. Has that changed even though you diverged artistically?**

No. We helped each other out. George and Marcia Lucas came down when I had a rough cut of *The Wind and the Lion* and made some suggestions, and then Marcia changed some things around. We all did this before we were rich. I mean, "rich," to me was $100,000; it wasn't like the millions that people had later. Before anybody had any money, everybody worked on each other's stuff; it was sort of fun. When Steven asked me to do the speech in *Jaws* (q.v.), I never thought of asking him for money. It was just fun to do. I still think of it that way, if you can help somebody, if you can help Francis [Coppola] or someone like that whenever he needs it. When you're writing something you like, it should be easy, it should be exhilarating.

The Wind and the Lion *was a romantic film in an age when America—Vietnam, Watergate—was not romantic. Whatever possessed you to write it?*

I don't know. I just write what I want to see, and it seemed like a good idea at the time, and it turns out that it *has* been a good idea. When I was on the PR tour, a film critic who was very, very liberal and snide and nasty came to me and said, "Why did you make this movie that has no relevance whatsoever with what we are?" I said, "What's a movie that's relevant?" He said, "*American Graffiti—that's* relevant to our lives." And I said, "What can I say to someone like you? You've never spent a night out of doors."

Big Wednesday

Nat Segaloff: **Big Wednesday**[25] *is a film that people either love or hate. I am one of the former, but the studio and the critics were among the latter.*

John Milius: Well, that film, you know, I just worked on it and that kind of evolved in a kind of organic way. I don't know how to regard it because the film was so viciously attacked at the time, and now people are beginning to like it a little more. It's sort of a numb spot in my life, still. I haven't gone back to look at it very often. It was a very personal film and it really tore me up that it was attacked in such a way that no one saw it. I would like to have communicated the things in that film to more people, but, I guess, if you can communicate with a few, you're successful. I showed that at the University of Chicago and a bunch of football players from Nebraska came down. They had all seen it many times and they wanted to thank me for making this film that was about friendship and it really moved them. There's this little cult of corn-fed football players that loved *Big Wednesday*. It was really moving to me because that's it. You don't get any reward, nobody's going to enshrine you and tell you how smart you are.

Someone told me, well, you see, John fell in love during that film, and that's what changed him.

---

25 The friendship of three "big name" California surfers—Matt Johnson (Jan-Michael Vincent), Jack Barlow (William Katt) and Leroy Smith (Gary Busey)—survives drinking, war, aging, and Nature itself during America's turbulent years 1962-1974.

That's true. That's really true. It really softened my life. I was gonna do a very harsh movie, and when I met Celia [his second wife] I decided I wanted to [make] a very heartfelt movie. I figured that was the last time that I could do that kind of thing. I really risked a lot. I felt I stretched a lot. I think it was really good for me. I think that even the beating I took was very good for me. I feel I'm much more immune to criticism.

The film stresses the passage of human time set against the ocean, which has no sense of time. You write about the importance of friendship and tradition in a youth-driven culture that constantly renews itself and forgets its forbears.

That's true. I had a great experience this summer. I went out and was surfing, and had gone a couple of times, and the surf was pretty good, and I saw the whole crew—Denny Aaberg, who co-wrote the script, and Lance Carson, who the script was about, and I saw everybody there. It was like a *Big Wednesday* reunion. Reb Brown, who plays the Enforcer, has become that character for real in life. He goes to Malibu and he kind of keeps order. It was a hot day, a hot weekend, and the surf had gotten good—it rarely does any more—and everybody was there. Everybody needed it.

Who is it who narrates the film?

It's a character named Fly, played Robert Englund,[26] a wonderful actor. He's one of the guys at the farewell party who says goodbye to Jack.

It's a beloved film now, but at the time it was not; I read the reviews. It was your first flop.

---

26 Later known as Freddy Krueger in the *Nightmare on Elm Street* films. A trivia note is that, although his character is present and narrates *Big Wednesday*, he has only one line of dialogue: "Stay casual, Barlow."

There was always a core group of young people in all kinds of places that liked and understood it. There was always a fanatical group that loved *Big Wednesday*, and they maybe saw it better than I did. *Big Wednesday* was one of those great Hollywood stories where about 97 percent of my friends abandoned me afterwards, you know, and I couldn't get any of my friends on the phone. Not the surfing friends, the Hollywood friends.

You were anathema because—

— it had *failed*. That was worse than anything. It was like having the plague. Nobody wanted to be anywhere *near* you because they were afraid they might catch it.

A film about friendship drove friends away.

Yeah. And I must say that I hardened; I was so completely disturbed. It came out at the same time as *Saturday Night Fever*, and...I couldn't understand why my film was scorned and I was so excoriated. I felt terrible. I was attacked for my hubris for daring to make a film like this that was about *surfers*. To have the Arthurian legend about surfers, and how horrible surfers were and how arrogant it was of me. I remember one night seriously considering joining the French Foreign Legion, but I didn't know whether I should fly to Marseilles in First Class or Coach.

As Bear tells Matt Johnson in the film, "Before the gods confer greatness upon a man, they test him." And also, "When you're wrong, that's when you need friends. When you're right, you don't need shit."

Yeah. It started out as a novel, you know.

You alone, or you and Denny Aaberg?

Just me. I wrote a good part of it, a quarter of it or so, the whole beginning. Not the novelization that was published. It was written in a very Steinbeck style.

How much does the film have to do with Denny Aaberg's short story "No Pants Mance"?

Not much, other than Denny was around and we both sort of idolized Lance Carson. He's the Jan-Michael Vincent character. Lance is a wonderful person and he's still a very close friend. He's a marvelous character because life did not follow art in his case. He was asked to participate in *Big Wednesday* and surf in it, but he was out of shape and an alcoholic. He made my boards for me and he made a few boards for other people, but his life was just a mess. Perhaps he saw—through the script, before the movie was finished—that his own life was pretty bad, and what he'd become. He went home one night and stopped drinking, without the need of AA or anything or anybody else, never took a drink again, and has lived a very, very productive life and become a wonderful piece of surfing legend, is in great health today and is still a great surfer. He hasn't had a drink since then and did it all by himself. Whereas Jan-Michael did the opposite; he played this character, and he then sank into a more spiraling decline.[27]

Was it difficult to configure modern characters in the mold of classic gladiators?

No, because I saw Malibu that way when I was growing up. I saw that it was a microcosm of the historical and the real world. You'd see the rise and fall of great men, empires built and lost, and all of this was done within the Pit [where the Big Name surfers hung out]. The years from the time I was, say, 12 until I was, say, 22 or 23—when I was forced to go inland, which is what

---

[27] Vincent struggled for years with substance abuse and run-ins with the law. He died in 2019 at age 74 (see Afterword).

happens to you when you walk back through that gate—I saw this happen. I saw an enormous amount of drama take place. These were colorful characters and there was a great deal of social change: the coming of hippies, the coming of drugs, the Vietnam war, the protests, the commercialization of surfing, the cheap heroes and the real heroes, the loss of morality, the pioneers being forgotten. All of that happened by the time I was 21 years old.

The passing of youth is vivid in the film-within-a-film, Liquid Dreams, the Endless Summer-type documentary that is screened for the surf community. Matt Johnson is crushed when the young audience has no idea who he was, but cheers for the new kid, Gerry Lopez.

And, of course, Gerry Lopez is a really good thing. He is the next generation; the torch has to be passed to him. At the end of the movie, Matt, Jack and Leroy say, "He's as good as they said he was."

With leadership comes responsibility, which is a frequent theme for you, and there's an exchange that talks about that in Bear's surfboard shop. Matt Johnson gripes that he doesn't want "a bunch of dorky kids" looking up to him but Bear says, "These kids look up to you whether you like it or not." That's the curse of anybody in a leadership capacity.

They bear the burden of leadership.

Was Matt ready for it?

No, no. He really wasn't ready for it till Big Wednesday. He was just a kid; he doesn't get the power to be a man until Bear gives him the big wave board the night before Big Wednesday.

At the end, Matt gives the sacred surfboard to some random kid instead of Lopez. Why?

Because Lopez is already "there." He doesn't need a board. The other kid needs the board. Gerry is Roland of France; he's swinging the sword Durendal. But the sword Excalibur must be passed on to another Englishman. If the kid doesn't deserve it, if he isn't worthy, he won't be able to ride it. He won't be able to pull it from the stone. Matter of fact, in the first version of the script—there were several versions—the board was floating, and that's how they first found it. What happens sometimes in really big surf, particularly at a place like Sunset or the Overhead, which are big surf spots, a tremendous riptide develops. A rip goes along sideways, but then it has to go back out to sea. And often a board might get into the rip and float out to sea. I was torn by the idea of having that happen, of having them stand there and watch it go back out to sea, like the Lady in the Lake.

Early in the film Sally (Patti D'Arbanville) muses, "Back home, being young was just something you did until you grew up, but here it's everything." In light of how civilization has turned its reins over to young people, does that line stand any differently?

I've always thought it was fascinating how, in California, youth is so valuable, we have a teenage culture. If you go to some place like New Orleans everything is keyed to adult culture. Way back when I was 14 or 15 years old, I remember going there to visit a friend, and he showed me Bourbon Street, where there were whores walking along. If we'd gone to one of the whores and said, "I want a try," she'd have said, "Get out of here, kid, come back when you're old enough." The bars where Dixieland was playing was a world that was closed to kids. I remember going into a private home and looking at this guy's quail dogs that he was raising, and the dogs were pointing the quail, and this was all something you had to grow up to have: a quail dog and a good shotgun. You had to go out and make a good living so you could have these things, whereas here [in California] it was all geared to youth and surfing, particularly. Your skin is bronzed, you're incredibly fit, and you have more time on your hands than maybe you should have, and no responsibilities. You can be a hero, like a high school football hero, but it's maybe even more seductive because, with a high school football hero, the season ends, and maybe he doesn't play in college, and that's the end of him—the glory of making that touchdown and his girl coming up to him in the end. But you can continue the surfing life for a long time. You can be the bronzed god out there with no money, living in your car, going with some actress who's rented a house in Malibu—of course, in those days, girls could rent those dives in Malibu; you can't any more, you have to be very rich— you could be this physical masterpiece of youth and vitality and all of this, and you could keep that going for a number of years and avoid real life and work, and questions of life.

Did you ever piss in anybody's steam iron as Matt Johnson apologized for doing?

No, but supposedly Lance Carson said that. He said that to Mrs. Aaberg. That's a true thing. He said, "I don't know who'd-a done it if I didn't do it, but I didn't do it. I swear I didn't do it. Somebody did it, but it wasn't me."

There's a symmetry in the two brawls in the first half of the film, one with crashers in Mrs. Barlow's house, and one in the bar in Tijuana.

The first brawl is innocent. Even though the fighting is brutal, and there's a very brutal punch where a crasher punches through a watermelon and hits Jan-Michael, it's violence, but it's cowboy violence, it's Roy Rogers violence, it's John Wayne violence. The fight in Mexico is real violence; it's the real world. People are shot, bottles smashed into girls' faces. That happened to me; I was a real tough character in Malibu. I could fight anybody, I knew jujitsu, I was a big guy, and I thought I was really tough. Well, surfers aren't tough. They're physically fit, but they're not tough. People who live in East L.A. and Watts, who have to struggle in the 'hood, *those* are tough people. Surfers think they are tough because they have great physical prowess, but they are not really tough. They're not tough-minded and they are not tough people. I remember when I spent the winter in Hawaii when I was 18, I thought I was a mountain man, I thought I was Jim Bridger. Then I saw real violence and real life, how dangerous it was. Even big wave riding was dangerous; you could be killed. The whole thing was terrifying and it made me realize that I wasn't at all what I thought I was.

That's the year you wandered into a cinema and saw the Kurosawa festival?

Yes.

You made Big Wednesday when you were 33, at a time in your life when you knew you could still do it.

I made *Big Wednesday* when I was still a world-class surfer and I could still rip. Aside from anything else, I knew it would be my swan song at Sunset Beach. But the memories were still fresh enough and the surfers were still there to talk to. So many of them have died since. But it was still possible to live and to feel that life a little bit. Had I waited five more years, that life would have drifted away. I wasn't cynical when I made it. I was still young enough to still believe much of what the film believes in. I don't think I could get away with it now. It was even a failure at the time. When Steven [Spielberg] saw it, he said, "You should have made it like *Animal House*."

Jan-Michael Vincent has said that doing the film killed the joy of surfing for him.

He probably says that because he wasn't that good a surfer. We had to have doubles. He could do little pieces of it, but that was it. So it probably made him aware of his shortcomings. Whereas, to me, I liked the fact that I could sit there just before dusk, when it was too late to match anything we'd shot, I'd say, "Everybody out of the water. The director wishes to have at least five or six waves to himself." And they'd all get out of the water and stand there and say, "Well, let's see him." And, of course, the old man could rip.

Is* Big Wednesday *the first truly authentic surf movie that didn't use blue screen and really had people in the water?

I think so. We wanted to show the wipeout and what happens to you. People say it's successful. To me it's not claustrophobic; it looks much too blue and nice, but you do get a little of the sense of being trapped.

The end sequence where Matt gets tubed—enclosed in curving wall of roiling water—is intense. There's blood and you flatten the sound.

You're trapped there. You can't get up. You're held down. Often when that happens it's dark. There's too much foam for light to get through. We couldn't show that, but it's quite terrifying. You're cut off from the world; nobody can help you. Surfing builds such friendships, and you try to watch out for each other, but there's really nothing you can do. You see your friend take a terrible wipeout off a twenty foot wave, there's nothing you can do. You can't go get him. What's interesting in that movie is that [Leroy and Jack] do get to go save [Matt], which is probably a romantization. Your chance of finding somebody under water after a wipeout like that is pretty slim.

At the end, when they climb the stairs and go back out through the gate, Matt is limping. In the script it says, "His leg is probably broken." Not is broken; probably broken. You leave a question.

That last sequence is really good in the script. I really like the way that was written. It's very Melvillean. That whole last section where the seagulls are churning above him, and they're all waiting. You really get a sense that he's going out there, passing set after set, waiting for that one wave. That film was in the days when you could make what you wanted. Nobody said that scene doesn't work. I mean, there were scenes that got taken out.

Did you take them out?

The studio did, but basically they didn't change the movie that much. Nobody said it should have a happier ending, or "Who are we rooting for here?" or "Who's the villain in the movie; can't we have a guy who's a bad Nazi surfer who grows up with them and has a duel in the end with Matt, and Matt finally wins and shows him up?" or that kind of shit. Or that Gerry Lopez should be some evil guy who's come to take over.

Are you responsible for Summer of Innocence?

I don't even know what *Summer of Innocence* is.

That's the hour-and-a-half version of Big Wednesday *that ABC ran on their network movie. You've never seen it?*

Obviously not.

The presence of Hank Worden (as "Shopping Cart") in Big Wednesday, *and Ben Johnson in* Dillinger *and* Red Dawn— *well-known veterans of John Ford films. Did you ever meet Ford?*

I met him at USC when he was old; he died shortly after that. I did have a great earlier encounter with him, though, that winter I spent in Hawaii. I would surf there till dark and paddle back at night, half a mile from the reef, thinking of sharks the whole time, of course. There was a great boat moored in Ala Moana Yacht Harbor with lights on it; it was John Ford's yacht (the *Araner*) and they were preparing to go off to do *Donovan's Reef*. I told them, "I'd like to hire on. I'll do anything I can." They said, "Do you know how to sail a boat? Are you a decent sailor?" I said, "No, but I can dive with the best of 'em and I can swim really good and I'm a great surfer and I really know the sea that way, but I've never sailed." And then John Wayne turned around and said, "Well, come back when ya *do* know how to sail, kid." John Ford and John Wayne were sitting there! John Ford says, "Sorry, kid, we don't have any surfing in this movie." I said, "Thank you very much, Mister Wayne and Mister Ford," and I went on my way. I look back at it now as a scene out of a movie. That didn't happen by accident, now did it?

Does a complete cut of Big Wednesday exist anywhere?

There was a pretty much complete cut, one that had Bear's story of what "Big Wednesday" is. The trims are still at Warner Bros. Hopefully, when they make the DVD, they'll let me put 'em back on.[28]

---

28 The author tried—unsuccessfully—to get Warner Bros. Home Video to restore the film in a Special Edition DVD.

Writing Other People's Movies

Nat Segaloff: There's been more written about the making of Apocalypse Now *than about Vietnam itself, and there were many similarities. I suppose you've already answered every question in the world about it.*

John Milius: I usually answer 'em different each time. I usually lie.

Your script[29] opens on Kurtz, whereas both the film and the book build up to Willard's encounter with him. Why did you choose to begin with Kurtz?

I just thought you had to see these guys. I wasn't really that concerned with staying at all in the tradition of the book. Matter of fact, I read the book when I was 16 years old and never read it again completely, except that I pick it up now and again and read parts of it, just open it up and start reading till I get tired. It's a very stilted book; in all of Conrad's work it's the most difficult to read, there's a certain disjointed quality about the sentences.

It's a story of a story, and it's distancing.

---

29 *Apocalypse Now*, based on Joseph Conrad's *Heart of Darkness*, was originally written in 1969 for George Lucas to direct when Francis Ford Coppola had Warner Bros.' backing for his visionary American Zoetrope company. Milius transposed Conrad's story of an ivory trader gone mad in the Congo into an allegory about the madness of Vietnam.

Not an easy-flowing *Nostromo*. Even *Lord Jim* is much easier to read. But when I read it the effect on me was so indelible that I never wanted to read it again. It was like *The Searchers* where, after I hadn't seen it for a while, I began to think I had dreamed it. The same thing with *Heart of Darkness*. I didn't want to go back and find the direct details, but it was amazing how much I'd remembered.

Why is *Kurtz* Kurtz but *Marlow* becomes Willard?

I wanted to use the name *Kurtz* because I wanted there to be no mistake that this was an allegory.

Kurtz *means "short" in German.*

Yeah, but I didn't pay any attention to that.

Martin Sheen said that he gave his character, B. L. Willard, the first name "Ben" because of the movie Willard. Ben was a rat.

The person the character's based on is Fred Rexer, who's always spiritual advisor on my films. He was [with the] Special Operations Group...and did things like that. The polio story[30] in *Apocalypse Now* happened to him. That was his village.

In Heart of Darkness, *Kurtz* isn't terribly concerned about the elephants he had to kill to get the ivory, but in Apocalypse Now *Kurtz* is very protective of the natives. Why the change from cavalier to compassionate?

As I remember, when you finally get to Kurtz in *Heart of Darkness* he's delirious and he doesn't even tell them much. They put him on the boat and leave, and he dies on the boat having said almost nothing. He never explains himself at all except that he

---

30 In which Kurtz relates how NVA soldiers chopped the arms off the kids that the American army had vaccinated.

says, "The horror." It's all Marlow explaining *about* him. So we had to have a different ending. Of course, I wrote the script years before the movie was made, but when I was writing it I knew that we had to have him explain himself. And he *does* explain himself, perhaps more than he should; it became his obsession.

As he leads Willard through his compound, he explains the meaning of patience and dedication in a very eastern way.

And if you go through all the versions, that continues. Kurtz, in the first version, is very different from the Kurtz in the last version, but there is a similarity. There's some wonderful stuff that was added, and stuff that was taken out, that was. When Kurtz is reading T.S. Elliot, Francis put that in because he wanted to sound literate: "We are the hollow men." Whereas what he *really* was saying there was that he was talking about the great hunt of the Mongols—that I took out and put in *Red Dawn*—about the circle that starts in a great area and then closes, and all the animals are driven forward, and the killing begins, and it becomes a slaughter, and nothing is allowed to get out of the circle. Finally, the young son of the Khan tugs on his father's sleeve and says, "Let those who are left go free." That really fits better.

In your script, Willard and his men stay in Kurtz's compound at the end as the NVA attacks, continuing the cycle of madness, and Willard, in effect, becomes Kurtz. In the film, they leave on the boat.

There were many different endings. There was one that was quite good in which Willard kidnaps Kurtz and takes him back to the boat where he and the crew escape back down the river, very much like *Heart of Darkness*, and the Montagnards follow, singing "Light My Fire," and ambush him. And after they ambush him, Willard calls in the air strike on himself.

How does it feel when a script you write takes on a life of its own halfway around the world, and you aren't there?

Most of the time you don't have somebody like Francis Coppola directing. He's a genius on a par with Orson Welles. Francis is the shining light of our generation. He's far and away the best filmmaker of our generation, and I think that's largely been forgotten. The rest of us are very good filmmakers, but Francis cut new ground. *Schindler's List* (Steven Spielberg, 1993) is a great film; *Raging Bull* (Martin Scorsese, 1980) is a great film. But Francis made *Apocalypse* and *The Godfather* (1972), and that's all he has to make. Those films are extraordinary masterpieces. You can look at the others and say, "This one's a failure, this one isn't that good, this one's great, this one's not, *Rumblefish* (1983) is a great film but it's not the size and power of those, *Peggy Sue Got Married* (1986) is a rather so-so film, *Tucker* (1988) is okay." But they fade to insignificance compared to *The Godfather* and *Apocalypse*. It just doesn't matter.

What the hell is Brando talking about in his colloquy?

He's trying to justify, explain to Willard what Truth is. He's trying to make him look into the pit and see the Truth, that he's looked in and seen the truth. He describes the whole thing about the V.C. and how they fight—they are capable of this barbarity, but they fight with passion. They have concern for the children. If we had 15 divisions like them, our troubles would be over. They're not fighting a lie.[31] One of the things about the Vietnam war that was terrible is that it was a lie between the President and the grunt. Prior to that, wars were not a lie between the

---

31 The meaning was clarified when *Apocalypse Now Redux* was released in 2001, restoring a major plot point in which Kurtz had warned the Joint Chiefs, in an intelligence report which they suppressed, that "dilettantes" on one-year tours of duty were useless against such a dedicated enemy as the NVA. This disillusionment leads directly to Kurtz's spiritual surrender to Willard. In 2019 Coppola released *Apocalypse Now: Final Cut* that clarified plot points. Milius feels it's the best of the many versions.

President and the grunt; people knew what they were fighting for. Fred Rexer said that this generation, which was capable of the kind of heroism that he experienced when he was there in '65 and '66, will "never be again purchased so cheaply." In other words, you used up, not just a generation, but a nation's ideals. And perhaps that's at the root of a lot of our problems.

Apocalypse Now *became the magnet for everybody's passion over Vietnam. You even took flack for things you had nothing to do with.*

I think you eventually figure that you're not doing movies to please everybody. What really made the difference to me was that, when I saw *Apocalypse Now,* all of a sudden the criticism didn't bother me. When I was being blamed for things in the movie rather than Francis, or whatever, I didn't care any more. I simply realized that the whole thing was larger than that, that the things which were dealt with in that movie were very important to me and were very important to a lot of people, and that it didn't matter whether someone liked it or not. Certain people had come up to me and said, "I was in the first Air Cav and, boy, I was really touched and moved. I felt like I was right back there." And other people came and said, "I was there for two years and I never saw a helicopter attack that was quite like that." And I'd say, well, I'm sorry we didn't do *your* Vietnam, we did somebody *else's* Vietnam." I would read reviews which were just ridiculous, where critics had obviously read the college outline series on Joseph Conrad and were pretending to have read *Heart of Darkness* and had obviously *not* read *Heart of Darkness.* Finally I realized that none of it matters. You just can't sit there and worry what some guy says one day. It's like somebody saying, "I don't like your kids." You say, "Well, that's too bad you don't like my kids. You have to live with them, too. They're in the world and you're in the world so tough crap."

Is that the kind of character you try to be?

I'm *supposed* to be the kind of character that says, "piss on 'em," but when somebody attacks you about your work, you get hurt, and gradually you get over it. Now I don't even think I get hurt any more, so (chuckles) maybe I *am* getting to be the kind of character who can say, "piss on 'em."

For all the notoriety of Apocalypse Now, you did some writing without credit that brought you equal notoriety: the Indianapolis speech from Jaws (Steven Spielberg, 1975).

The reason that scene is so important and works so well is because you use your imagination. But you need a really good actor to pull it off.

Did you really write that with the phone off the hook while Steven Spielberg waited on the other end on Martha's Vineyard?

Yeah, but it was two phone calls. He called me several days before and said to be prepared to write something about why this guy doesn't like sharks. Steven and I have a long history of his exploitation of me.

Did you immediately think of the Indianapolis incident?

I thought of several. There were two other incidents, both of them involving the area around the Solomons. In the Battle of Iron Bottom Sound there were a lot of people eaten by sharks. Then there was the battle of the Bismarck Sea in which Japanese transports were machine-gunned, strafed, by B-25s and P-38s and the sea was filled with corpses and bodies, and live people trying to swim to shore, and the sharks had a feast. The Americans flying over were sickened by it.

Was Robert Shaw actually drunk shooting the scene, as has been said?

He was totally drunk. As Steven tells it, he'd been caught by his wife screwing the nanny. So in the middle of the thing he'd be talking about, "You ever seen a shark's eyes? Cold and dead, and turns over just like when your wife tells you you've been screwing the nanny." Steven would say, "No, Robert, you're drifting." Or "So many people bobbin' in the water. They was caught by their wives, too." They shot it the day it was written. Sometimes things happen quickly and you don't think much about it at the time, and for the rest of your life you're talking about it and being asked about it.

Between the Indianapolis speech, the "I know what you're thinkin'" speech from Dirty Harry, and "I love the smell of Napalm in the morning" from Apocalypse, you may be remembered for things that aren't in your own movies.

Well, if I can be remembered for a few good speeches, that's all right.

Even in The Hunt for Red October (John McTiernan, 1990) you were called in to rewrite Sean Connery's dialogue, but it must have been more complicated than that.

Just to rewrite all the Russian stuff.

The other dialogue in the scene, too, or only Connery's lines?

I could write anything that was Russian scenes. I asked if I could do the American stuff and he said, "no."

You and Spielberg executive produced two films by Bob Gale and Robert Zemeckis (I Wanna Hold Your Hand, 1978 and Used Cars,[32] 1980) and then Spielberg directed their

---

[32] I Wanna Hold Your Hand exuberantly follows the adventures of a group of kids trying to see The Beatles on The Ed Sullivan Show in 1964; Used Cars is about try-anything salesmen plying their trade.

script, from your story, 1941.[33] *It may be his worst film. What happened?*

It felt of too much, just the wrong approach. Steve was the wrong director. It's just not the type of movie that he should have done. It should have been a small, contained movie that had its roots in real experience. And if you overdo everything and make it the biggest this and the biggest that, you lose the real experience. Everything in *Used Cars* comes out of a reality; nothing in *1941* came out of a reality, though the original script was very well rooted in reality. It was a real incident that actually happened. A lot of funny things happened, and it was so twisted by the time that it got on the screen that it lost that. So the problem really comes back down to a regard for writing. I maintain that the fault of that movie can be blamed on the director's interpretation of the script.

What was it like being a producer? On Used Cars *or* I Wanna Hold Your Hand, *could you or Spielberg have fired the director and taken over?*

We couldn't do that because there's a rule that the Directors Guild passed. It's referred to as the "Clint Eastwood clause" because he once took over one of his movies from another director.[34] As a matter of fact, on *Used Cars*, when Steven was out of town, they called me in and I went down and got them back on budget—gave them "a stern talking-to." I told [Robert Zemeckis] he'd gone over budget and that was dishonorable. He said, "Yeah, but what are you supposed to do when you go over budget and it's not your fault? If it rains?" I said, "Bob, if you go over budget, rain, shine, whatever—there's always the knife." He said, "What do you mean?" I said, "Seppuku, Bob. It's dishonorable to go over budget. Those guys on Tarawa, it wasn't their fault that twenty thousand Marines landed, but

---

33 A comedy based on the fallacious sighting of a Japanese submarine off the shore of California shortly after Pearl Harbor.
34 Phillip Kaufman began *The Outlaw Josey Wales*, 1976.

they still lost the battle." Going over budget is an offense that can only be reconciled with Hara-kiri.

I can think of a lot loftier ideals to take one's life than going over budget.

But you've got to think that way or else you don't discipline yourself.

Usually money buys everything in Hollywood, not just movies.

You've heard all kinds talk about the "fools that run the studios" or the "fool producers," the dishonorable, rotten people. Some of them truly are all of that. But, at the same time, I always had very high regard for the fact that they're people who give you the money and the responsibility to do a job, and, as a professional, you owe them your word to do that job. So I do the best I can to give 'em their money's worth and not spend more. I'm really honored each time they let me go out. I can call them fools and dolts creatively, but I can't break that discipline that they've put upon me. It's a matter of honor. As a professional I've given my word that I will do this job. Did j'ever read *The Song of Roland?*[35] Roland is defending a pass [on August 15, 778] against 100,000 Saracens and he's got 20,000 French. He can have Oliver, his best friend, blow on a horn and call Charlemagne back through the pass at Ronceveaux and probably save him. But, he says, "It is the pride of what we are that we shall oppose them with only what we have." Of course, they're slaughtered to a man. But what a way to go! And it was honorable.

---

35 The epic quaternary, believed to have been written by the poet Turoldus in the eleventh century, which chronicles the life and battles of William the Conqueror and his Emperor Charlemagne.

Conan the Barbarian

***Nat Segaloff:** When you made* Conan the Barbarian *in 1981 you sort of created Arnold Schwarzenegger, didn't you?*

John Milius: Arnold was already there. He was a movie star, he was a character. When I was trying to talk Dino DeLaurentiis into using him, I said that if we didn't *have* Arnold we'd have to *build* him. It's like that line in *Lawrence of Arabia*: "Aqaba is there, we only have to go."

The script had a torturous development—previous drafts by Ed Summer & Roy Thomas, then Oliver Stone and L. Sprague van de Camp. What elements did you introduce?

What was done up till then wasn't usable. It was a fever dream, it wasn't *Conan*. I took the things out of R. E. Howard that I wanted to use and picked a primal story of revenge. I had the idea of doing a trilogy.[36] The first one would be about strength—"that which does not kill you makes you stronger"—and in the end, Thulsa Doom tells him the truth. He says, "I'm the reason you're strong. I'm the reason you're here. I'm the reason you're Conan. What will your world be without me?" Then Conan kills Thulsa Doom—which he must do, or Thulsa Doom will kill him—and then he doesn't know what to do next. So he contemplates, "Where do I go? Now that I'm built, now that I'm a strong, completed man, what do I do? Where do I go?" I love

---

[36] There were two ersatz Conan sequels, *Conan the Destroyer* (1984) and *Red Sonja* (1985). Plans for a revival, *King Conan*, were announced in 2000. See the Afterword.

the ending we put back [for the DVD, in which Conan returns the kidnapped princess to her kingdom] in which he says that he will return her and not let her pray to me, because I am not a god, I am just a man. She will not bow to false idols. I will not have that; there is only one God." He's free, but—and this is something that is echoed in a lot of my films—free do to what?

Did you refer to Fritz Lang's Neibelungen[37] *saga?*

I never saw the *Neibelungen* saga. I've read *The Ring of the Neibelungen*, a lot of Icelandic sagas, and things like *Beowulf*. Primitive Nordic stuff. I would say this is very strongly couched in those.

Executive Producer Dino DeLaurentiis[38] was known for making big-budget films despite being frugal. How much rewriting had to do with budget?

The first time I rewrote it, the budget was too high [$19 million estimate, considerable for 1980]. I had a huge battle with thousands of people and armies of mutant Neanderthals and that whole kind of thing. I took the battle out. Now the battle's between Conan and sort of a sidekick and twenty mutant Neanderthals—we could afford twenty mutant Neanderthals—but it's a better battle because it's more about *people*. I really got a kick out of solving a situation that way through my writing. The first battle, which I took out, would have been something that I could have appreciated, and probably would have been appreciated at West Point, since I was redoing particular classic battles, but I don't think it really fit in the movie very well.

When you take a character that is established in the pulps and comics and people know him, what responsibility do you have?

---

37 *Siegfried* (1923) and *Krimhild's Revenge* (1924).
38 By way of acknowledgement, the film was nurtured for years by producer Edward R. Pressman prior to DeLaurentiis's involvement.

You have to be faithful. I made a movie that I know Robert E. Howard would have loved. Francis once said something when we doing *Apocalypse*. He said, "When I made *The Godfather* I made it more like Mario Puzo than Mario Puzo. And this movie will be more like you than you."

Most movies made from comic book characters are awful.[39] Why does Conan work?

Conan doesn't take a comic book mentality. It doesn't even use comic book framing. It's not a light film. It's very Germanic. Somebody even said that this movie would have been very popular at the Nuremberg rallies in 1936.

We are 24 minutes into the film before even Conan has his first line of dialogue answering the question, "What is best in life—?"

"—To crush your enemies, to see them driven before you, to hear the lamentation of their women."

How did you make him accessible to the audience?

Basic emotions are always accessible to audiences and all of the things that Conan does, we all feel ourselves. He just acts upon them with more intensity than we do. I try to keep him as much of a barbarian as possible because it's true to the times. If I was making a movie about a character in the wild west he would be true to his time of 150 years ago, and he would certainly be a lot different than our time, but we should be able to relate to him. We should be able to relate just as easily to Conan.

How does Conan, being a barbarian, hold to the Milius sense of honor and humanity?

---

39 This was written well before the Marvel Universe nailed the formula, but I'm not absolutely persuaded that I'm not still right.

Well, Conan is a barbarian and most of his conflict is with evils that are wrought by civilization. He was a marvelous hero, like Achilles. He sulked and ran away and was forced into things and had great rages and great melancholies. He is a character who relies on the animal, and I always believe that the animal instincts in people are the better part of them, and that the civilizing instincts are often the worst part of them. It's kind of contrary to what everyone else says where they say, "Isn't it better to think and evolve" and all of this, and all I say is [that] all you do when you think and evolve is corrupt yourself sooner or later. When the going gets tough, the tough get feral.

As we do these interviews there's a chance that you will finally get to make your trilogy. Where does Conan go now, especially where Arnold is twenty years older?[40]

He'll play Conan as a king and a father. I read a lot of R. E. Howard and a lot of history, and I've read some other novels and things and I've gone over and looked at certain things and come to an understanding again of what the essence of Conan should be. I have to write about something that appears to me. Sometimes it doesn't make any sense.

How do you mean?

Well, sometimes I'll keep thinking of things. I'll say, "It should be like this" or "I really like this story" and I remember something in an old novel or movie. What is there about this story that I like? Obviously I can't do the same story, but there's something about this story that I like that resonates with Conan. If it keeps coming back and doesn't go away and no other story comes up, it's something that's there. It means something to me.

---

40 Alas, it didn't happen. See Afterword.

How close do you feel your first **Conan** *was to the Robert E. Howard Conan?*

Not really that close, but in spirit it was. I didn't follow any stories, and he had a lot more magic and supernatural. But it was really, in spirit, very close to Robert E. Howard. It very definitely followed the Robert E. Howard spirit. That's what I have to do here, too.

The first film doesn't rely on dialogue. Matter of fact, Arnold only has one exchange with Sandahl Bergman, and she's his co-star.

Conan is the movie where I finally said, "Yeah, now I think I really have learned my trade."

What was it like working with Dino DeLaurentiis?

That was really rough. He fought me on everything. He never understood the film.

So why did he want to produce it?

Because it was a deal, and Dino loved to deal. He liked to deal more than he liked to film. One thing I can say about Dino, whatever he did [and] despite his interference, he was a superb producer. I always had enough, more than enough.

Did he visit the set?

Oh, yeah, he visited the set. Threatened to fire me and everybody else several times. He didn't like me 'cause I opposed him. But anybody who went along with him and kissed his ass he just crushed. I suppose, you know, all my troubles in the end will build character. What doesn't kill you makes you stronger.

That's what the movie's all about. Conan had to spend time on the Wheel of Pain and I had to spend time with Dino.

Red Dawn

Nat Segaloff: In a lot of ways, Red Dawn—in which a group of teenagers defends America after Russia occupies the United States using conventional warfare—is an anti-nuclear film because it says that nuclear weapons are useless.

John Milius: It also says that World War Three is un-winnable. Or we're gonna win, but the cost is gonna be so great. I think it shows the utter futility, the desperate futility of war. At the end of the movie, in spite of all the heroism and valor shown and the reasons and the revenges on both sides, all that's left is a lonely plaque on some desolate battlefield that nobody goes to.

War is supposed to make heroes, but these kids don't really become heroes.

They become heroes and then they become animals. They become used up, just chewed up. There was a scene that was taken out that was important, but the studio wanted gone, where the kids shoot into a house and a little girl is in there and they almost kill her, and they realize that they, too, are guilty. They give her a little bit of food, and one of the kids says, "It would be better if we'd killed her."

You said that "making an anti-war film is like making an anti-rain film." Could you elaborate?

War is part of man's nature. We make war. We've always made war. We're not going to eradicate war. The act of eradicating war is war itself. There isn't a war film around that says war is glorious. The paradox of war is what's so interesting: as horrible as war is, people find it interesting because it's human drama. Drama is human abrasion, and war is the ultimate human abrasion.

An unusual number of your films involve moments in which two adversaries salute each other: the Cuban commander letting Patrick Swayze carry away Charlie Sheen in Red Dawn; *the Raisuli and the German swordsman square off in* The Wind and the Lion *as well as the Raisuli and President Roosevelt; Gerry Lopez and Matt Johnson in* Big Wednesday; *Johnson and the Crow fisherman in* Jeremiah Johnson; *Submarine Captains Sean Connery and Scott Glenn in* The Hunt for Red October; *Nick Nolte and Powers Boothe in* Extreme Prejudice; *and even Purvis and Dillinger in* Dillinger *and Kurtz and Willard in* Apocalypse Now. *In each of these encounters, there is a kinship between enemies.*

That's an acknowledgement that we have all suffered this battle together. You see it a lot in other movies; I just saw it in *Gladiator* when he fights off Sven and doesn't kill him, and you assume that Sven becomes one of his men at the end. It was very well done in *The Naked Prey* (Cornel Wilde, 1966) where the man becomes more and more ruthless chasing Cornel Wilde, even to the point where, the more of his men that are killed, the more he urges them on. He doesn't even get Wilde at the end; when Wilde gets to the fort he looks back and sees him there, and the guy goes [waves] and Wilde goes [waves]. That's a wonderful moment, that's what makes that film so good. It's a very good film.

Can war be for thinking people?

War is always for thinking people. The greatest minds in the world spend more time devising wars than anything else. As Patton says, compared to war all other human endeavor shrinks to insignificance. But that's also the fascination and the crime of war: that is uses up so much good energy of the human race, and the fact that it does use it up is the fascination, too. Lee said that "It is lucky war is such hell, lest we love it so." Alexander Haig was saying that war is utterly futile, but to prevent war is the job of the soldier, at least in America. It was interesting because this policy has worked. For whatever you have to say, we haven't had a war. We've had all the players and no game. You have to be strong enough so that aggressors will not—I mean, if you're a super power you have to take on the responsibilities of a super power. That's what he was saying, too. That situation will prevail that if you allow yourself to grow weak, somebody will take advantage of it[41]

When you were constructing Red Dawn, **what did you have to do to convince the audience to accept the possibility of an invasion on America soil?**[42]

The conventional war, the limited nuclear exchange, is something that we've been hearing a lot about in the news. I don't know if people have been paying attention to it, but all of these weapons that all of the furor in Europe is about—the Pershing Missile and the Cruise Missile—are low-yield tactical nuclear weapons. They are not strategic nuclear weapons, they're tactical nuclear weapons. The MX is a strategic weapon; that goes under the policy of mutually assured destruction. All these other things are for limited nuclear exchange. Well, that's an alarming prospect: limited nuclear exchange. It will lead to the type of war described in the movie.

---

41 This conversation was held before President George W. Bush went to war in Afghanistan in 2001 and in Iraq in 2003.
42 This conversation was conducted prior to the September 11, 2001 terrorist attacks on New York City and Washington, DC.

Kevin Reynolds' original script for what became* Red Dawn *was called* Ten Soldiers, *wasn't it?

It was a completed script. I changed a lot; I wanted to make it more real, and Kevin Reynolds' script was more of a meditation on the kids going bad, like *Lord of the Flies*. I loved the idea that this would really be happening, and taking a lot of stuff out of French and Russian Resistance stories, and that this war they're fighting is gonna use them up—and, in particular, their leader, Jed (Patrick Swayze), because more and more responsibility falls on his shoulders. They're not going to make a big difference, but the fact that they fought and they died makes a difference. Once again, you have that Mongol circle of death where they let the last living creatures go free. As Jed and his brother Matt (Charlie Sheen) get away, one says, "We're free now" and the other says, "Free?"

It was pretty cheeky making a war film without super-heroes like Arnold or Bruce or Sly or Clint.

I wanted to show this war on a very small unit basis, but, even further than that, among a very small group of people. Obviously there's a lot more going on outside them, a lot of groups resisting, giving in. I thought it was necessary, at one point in the story, to tell what was happening, to have the air force pilot (Powers Boothe) arrive and explain a few things about the big war. And then I felt it was necessary to see the big war on personal terms: that the kids' parents were killed; that the kids were trapped by the three Russians who were going to kill them, so they had to kill; and the Cuban commander has to kill these people because that's the only way to stop this, and it goes back and forth. You realize that war is like a great big machine that just grinds people up, nobody looks back, they're just shooting at each other across these great distances every day, airplanes and tanks, these steel machines that are exterminating each other. And when these kids get into this they realize they're immediately way over their heads. Finally Jed pays for it. He gets burned out.

So does the Cuban commander (Ron O'Neal), who makes a gallant gesture at the end and lets Jed carry off his wounded brother, Matt.

A man like that, a man of ideals when he started fighting, all of his wars were wars of national liberation where he was justified in freeing people from oppression—and finally he becomes the oppressor.

I recall the end of Apocalypse Now when somebody asks Willard, "did we win or did they just stop coming?"

Win or lose is a matter of luck. I go by the Viking philosophy that, in life, if you're a Viking, you are possessed of wonderful qualities of strength and courage and artistry. Every Viking was a poet, every Viking could play a musical instrument and sing, as well as fight like a Berserker and show the courage to launch a boat against the storm in the middle of winter. All of these things were accepted. But luck was something that the gods conferred, so they would always sing their songs about luck. They would talk about bad luck, and how somebody was really great, but as soon as he went out, the boat sank. They would talk about other bad luck where this guy went and pillaged the entire world and came back to Denmark and on a river was attacked by other Vikings who took everything from him, and the good luck of somebody who had survived this terrible storm with an ice beard, or survived a battle and lived to a great age, and tested himself by going Viking each year.

"Before the Gods confer greatness upon a man they test him" is a theme that runs through your films.

Gerry Lopez would take me to places. We'd be climbing down some hideous coral cliff to jump into the ocean when the big wave would come along and cover the coral up, coral like razor blades, and he'd say, "Now we jump." I'd say, "Gerry, I can't jump; I can't even get down a ladder." And he'd say, "We gotta do this. This will build character." That was his whole thing. That was Gerry's thing in life: whatever happens, down the line we're gonna benefit from it.

You received a special kind of approbation for Red Dawn, didn't you, other than the box office returns, which pretty much saved MGM's neck.

I showed Red Dawn at the Alexander Haig screening to a bunch of people who were in the War College—people who'd been to Vietnam, Colonels, Generals and stuff. These guys had all been in a real war, and their perspective is different from a movie critic's. They didn't say anything for a long time, and then a guy came up who'd gotten the Medal of Honor and thanked me for making the movie and said, "At least somebody understands what we are trying to do and why we are soldiers." Ultimately that's the only reward you ever get for doing something like this. Other rewards, of getting awards and money, are always hollow. I think of Warren Beatty, that he engineered all the respect he was going to get for Reds (1981) and he really didn't get any, did he? It didn't work. He got his Oscar® and everything else, but I don't think anybody comes up to him and said that they were really moved by Reds. Fame and glory and all those things are quite empty words.

Maybe that's why Ford and Hawks and Wellman and Dwan keep their characters silent.

Anything you do really well, it's hard to describe. There's a whole kind of Zen thing. A friend of mine is an unbelievable pilot and he's now gonna become a general. He said he read a briefing report that they're trying to show fighter pilots that everything you do well, you really can't discuss, you should just go with the instinct. When they asked Lynn Swan how to catch a pass, he said, "Well, I just jump up and catch it." If you sit down and try and define what something you did well or care about is, you kind of lose it.

How gracefully you tell the interviewer to ask another question.

No, I mean, when you sit there and try to imbue the thing, for example, with a spirit of the family, the way Ford did, he couldn't tell you what he did. And I don't even think he knew what he did. He just felt it and put it in the movie. If it feels right, that's the basic thing.

There are countless photos of John Milius and his films all over the Internet. This book presents background images that illuminate his work. All are from Wiki Commons unless otherwise noted.

Bob "The Emperor" Hudson (L) and Ron Landry, the morning team on Los Angeles radio, put their routines on comedy albums in the 1960s. Emperor Hudson was the subject of an early George Lucas film that Milius wrote.

The Southern California surfing culture -- part athlete, part delinquent -- as captured by photographer John Robert McPherson.

Photo Gallery

Robert Craig "Evel" Knievel, the bigger-than-life subject of Milius's screenplay for actor-producer (and self-confessed con man) George Hamilton.

John "Jeremiah" Johnson, a.k.a. "Liver-eatin' Johnson," for his peculiar dining habits. How a real mountain man ever sat still for a portrait is anybody's guess.

Judge Roy Bean, the self-installed "law west of the Pecos." "I know the law," Milius wrote as his dialogue, "having spent my entire life in its flagrant disregard."

President Theodore Roosevelt, the favorite Chief Executive of both John Milius and his father, William.

John Flammang Schrank who attempted to shoot President Theodore Roosevelt.

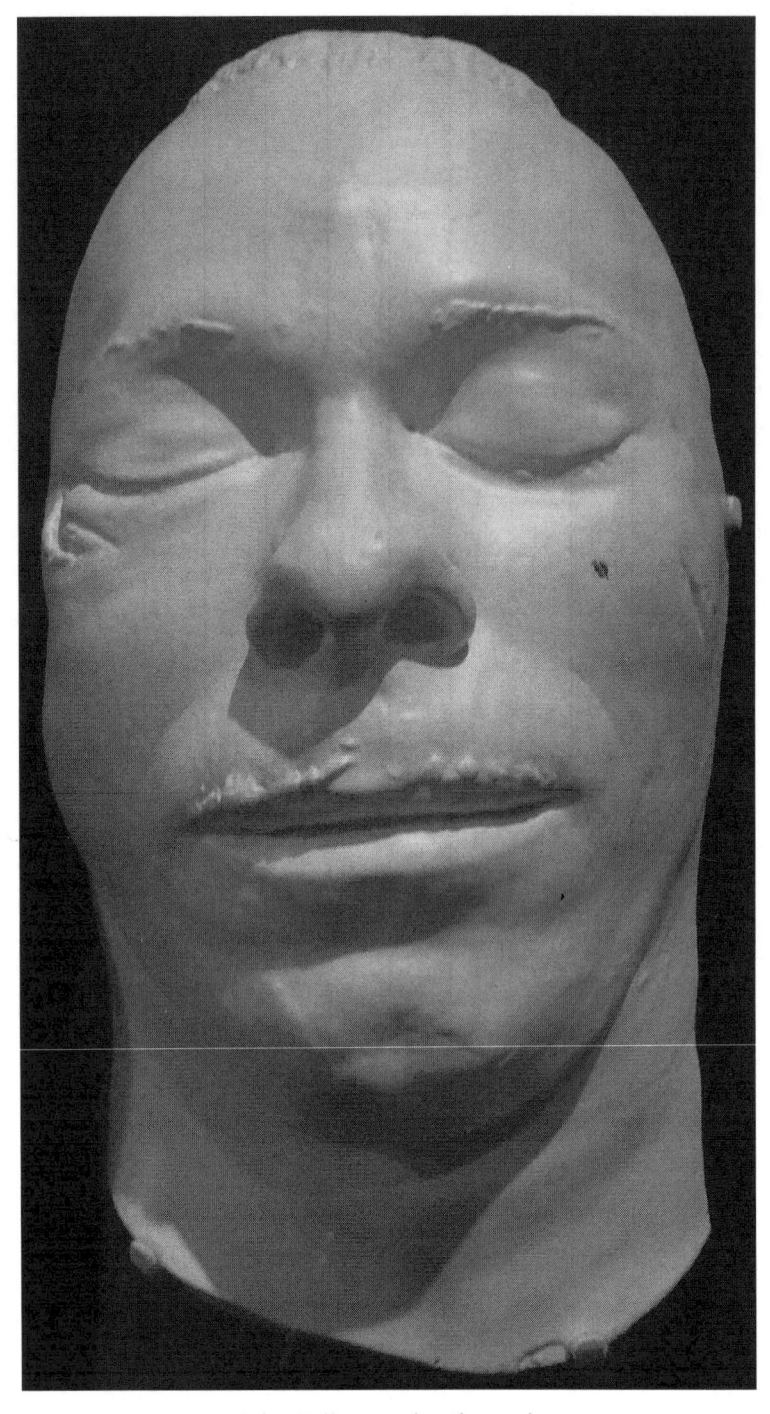

John Dillinger death mask.

Melvin Purvis, the G-Man who shot Dillinger and later took his own life with the same pistol.

Rosita Forbes, author of the book El Raisuni, Sultan of the Mountains, *which inspired* The Wind and the Lion. *(Credit: Mendoza)*

Mulai Ahmed el Raisuni, the real-life inspiration for Mulay Hamid el Raisuli, played by Sean Connery in The Wind and the Lion.

With Arnold Schwarzenegger on location in Spain for Conan the Barbarian *(Credit: Bob Penn/ George Whitear)*

With Nick Nolte for Farewell to the King. *(Credit: Hugh Van Es)*

The Rough Rider officers cited for gallantry in Cuba during the Spanish-American War. Top Row: Adjutant Keys, Lt Hayes, Capt. Woodbury Kane, Capt. Day, Surgeon James Church. Bottom Row: Lt. Ferguson, Lt. Goodrich, Capt. Franz, LtCol. Brodie, Theodore Roosevelt, Lt. John Campbell Greenway, Lt. Greenwald. (Credit: Harvard College Library)

On the desert location for The Wind and the Lion.

The image of Milius that many people think sums him up, yet really doesn't. Well, maybe a little.

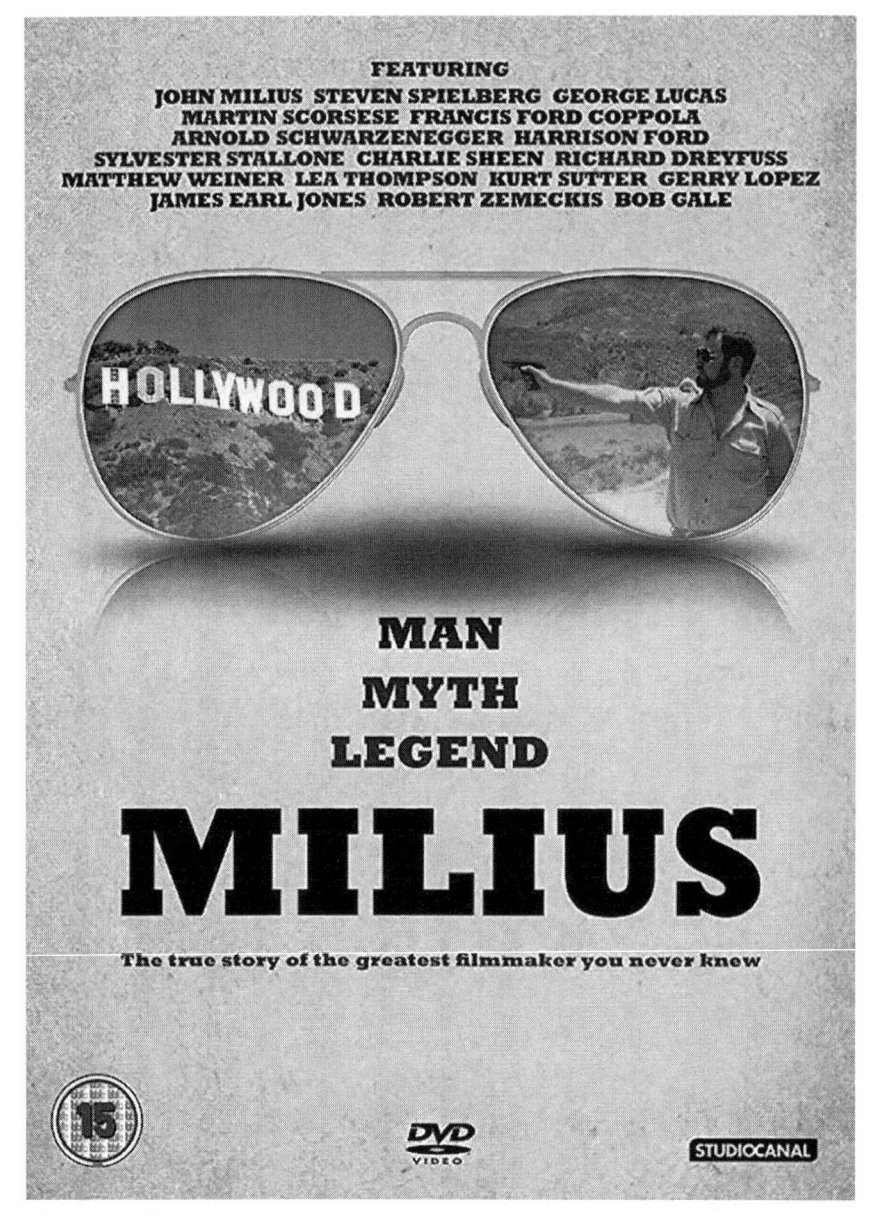

Poster for the affectionate 2013 documentary, Milius, subtitled "The True Story of Greatest Filmmaker You Never Knew."

Photo Gallery 87

(L-R) Gary Busey, William Katt, Lee Purcell, Darrell Fetty and (below) Jan-Michael Vincent at the 2019 Big Wednesday reunion in Los Angeles on June 1, 2019. (Credit: Denise Culp)

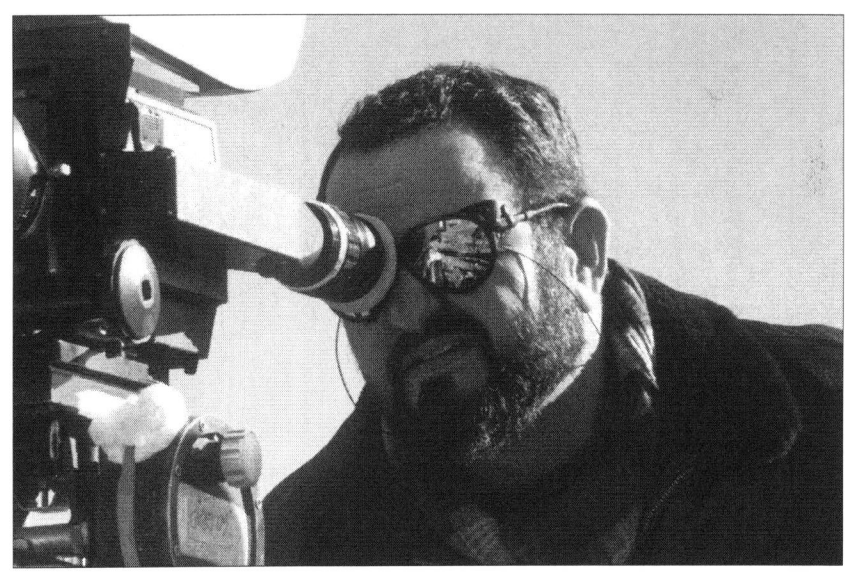

John looks through the eyepiece of a camera undisturbed by his mirrored shades. (credit: Jean Milius/ Wiki Commons)

General Curtis LeMay, the bombastic subject of Milius' as-yet-unproduced screenplay Patriotism *(nee M.A.D.: The Life and Times of Curtis LeMay).*

United States Aier Force crew on a training flight for the Son Tay prison raid (November 1970). (Credit: USAF)

Farewell to the King

Nat Segaloff: *Farewell to the King[43] is your David Lean film by way of Joseph Conrad.*

John Milius: There are some David Lean-esque things in it, some *Bridge on the River Kwai*—actually, more *Lawrence of Arabia*.

Nick Nolte once said how you kept on going deeper into the jungle, but I wasn't sure whether he was talking about you or the film.

I had a ball. I got to really like the jungle. I lost about 25 or 30 pounds while I was there (and gained it back). If there was a river to cross, I was the first one in. It's a great boy's adventure to go into the jungle and make a movie. It's pretty neat to be paid to go off and have adventures.

There's a more sweeping sense of the futility of war than in Red Dawn.

I've matured in that way, but the story certainly comes from a lot of time, reflection, and age. It does seem to be a lot different from earlier ones.

---

43 From the 1969 novel by Swiss journalist Pierre Schoendoerffer, the story follows Learoyd (Nick Nolte), a deserter in World War Two, who sets himself up as King of a South Pacific island by virtue of unifying its disparate Dayak tribes, then must face the Japanese anyway when war catches up with him.

You really are a monarchist, aren't you?
Naw, I'm an anarchist, but if I have to choose anything, it would be to serve a feudal lord.

Which, of course, is why you work in the studio system.

I work wherever they'll pay!

You've been quoted as following the code of the Bushido.

I've also been quoted that a lot of the principles by which I live were dead before I was born.

Why Bushi and not Samurai?

The Bushido is the code of the Samurai.

One has a master and the other doesn't.

One *must* have a master. One is best when serving a king. But, then, again, I've spent most of my life as a Ronin.

Unlike other movie action heroes, yours have a sense of their place in history, and of the hero myth itself. Learoyd (Nick Nolte) even gives himself up so his adoptive people can be free.

I like Learoyd [Nick Nolte] because he realizes that he's served his function as a legend, and that he, himself, the man, doesn't need anything. These people, as he says, will be strong because of the stories they'll tell *about* him, not *because* of him.

He speaks, as many of your characters do, in a classical style, even though the film is set in the 1940s, which is fairly contemporary.

I wanted him to speak as though he was used to speaking in a classical language because of the way the Dayaks speak. Their language is almost like Greek or Latin. If you translate their stories they are very Homeric. There is a certain formality in the way he speaks: "Solon the Terrible challenged me to fight, and it was my opportunity to become one of them. We fought and many blows were exchanged, and finally I prevailed." I forget exactly what he says, but it's a formal, stylized way of speaking.

There's a line that Schoendoerffer uses: "These were the days of high adventure." You even gave it to Mako in Conan the Barbarian.

I love that phrase.

There's the sense of the jungle being a character in the story.

That's what I wanted. I always try to do that in all my movies, have the place be a character, because I think that ultimately is important.

In Borneo you really feel you're in another world.

I try to do that. My style is geared to that. I never use any zooms or long lenses or anything. I just want a sense that you're there. When the camera moves, you should never really know it, other than that you feel excited or exhilarated by the movement. You should never know, God, you're moving on a camera. There's a lot more movement than you think if you look at it again; you just don't notice. We put track down in the jungle everywhere.

Location is especially important because you have fights between the factions of the Japanese, the British, Nolte's Dayak forces, and you need to know that they are in a thick jungle, that they can't just look across the trees and see each other. You have to know the terrain.

I like that big nightmare battle, the whole moment of the moon going behind the clouds and they lose the advantage of seeing them—and then they can't hear 'em any more—and then *there they are*. I think it's some of my best work. I like the way the movie looks and the way it's staged. I fought very hard for this movie.

Did your asthma bother you in the hot, humid jungle?

I don't have asthma any more. Elan [Oberon, who plays Vivienne opposite Nigel Havers] cured me. Made me cut out all dairy products. I used to have these asthma attacks from the time of *Dillinger* on, and then they just stopped. I went to a Dayak shaman in Borneo and he did things over me. Maybe took away all that. I believe in all things like that. Even though I'm Jewish by birth, I'm a practicing Pagan. I actually think the most sense of any religion is the Apache religion.

You start the film with a scene that isn't in the book, in which Learoyd first lands on the island and has the chance to shoot the Japanese Colonel, but he's shaking with fear and can't aim. Why did you feel you needed this?

The character of the Japanese Colonel wasn't revealed until almost the very end of the book, when [Learoyd and the tribes] started their war against the Japanese and then they found out there was this abandoned column and this Colonel. I wanted to reveal at the very beginning that this Colonel was a phantom, a larger-than-life figure that would come back to haunt Learoyd. He sees him in another place, too. I remember shooting him in some rocks when Learoyd was hiding under some rocks.

You once used an expression in speaking of Farewell to the King: "The ambiguities of being free." What does that mean?

Remember that he says, "I'm free, I'm free." Well, free to do what? Freedom brings with it a certain responsibility. You have to take care of yourself; you have to find something worthwhile to do. Freedom brings with it a lot of baggage that isn't necessarily what you expected.

Learoyd, an American, sets up an island monarchy and unifies the Dayak tribes, but it's unclear in the movie just how he does this.

In the movie it's unclear because they [Orion Pictures] took all that out. It was quite clear in the movie how he gets the women to have a sex strike and nobody gets laid until they come to the conference table, and all this kind of thing. He goes to the women and he uses them. Then he uses pride, the pride that they must be strong amongst themselves and unify, or the world will come in and get them. He's a great king.

What motivates him to want to do this? I don't remember it being clearly articulated in the book, either.

In the movie he decides to become king because he remembers the legend of the Round Table and he feels that they need to have this to protect themselves. He really does it totally out of generosity. He's not doing it for his own glory. He really wants to protect this place that he's found. He's had enough of the rest of the world. Learoyd is a man who has plans. That's one of the things that's in several of my scripts: "He had plans."

Speaking of "plans," the film was heavily cut and then barely released, wasn't it?

It was thrown away and not given any real launching or anything. I, as usual, was attacked viciously for it, but, in time, I think it's become regarded as one of my best. In a way, I don't know why, I guess this film is more heart-felt than anything since *Big Wednesday*.

Orion Pictures demanded cuts and changes after your director's previews, and the producers took their side.

The producers Al Ruddy and André Morgan—who are friends of mine now—were lied to by the Orion executives. They did a very careful divide-and-conquer and turned us against each other. They (Ruddy and Morgan) would love to recut it the way I wanted. Right now. We'd all love to recut that movie and re-release it.

Why would Orion have wanted to change your movie?

Why do they ruin scripts? The executives—out of, once again, stupidity—decided that they had a better idea.

Only after they saw the movie but not when they read the script?

The movie showed (previewed) very well, but they decided it had to be shorter and had to move at a quicker pace, and the movie failed because of it. You're only seeing about three quarters of the movie and you need that other quarter. It should be my favorite movie because my director's cut probably was one of my favorite movies. You can ask Steven [Spielberg]; he thought it was the best movie I ever made. He saw it in that edition and thought it was a masterpiece. There are some mistakes that I would do differently if I were going to do them now, that they talked me out of, that I would have insisted on. I would have had Learoyd be more of a rascal. One of the things he did was impregnate all the girls. As king he had lots of girls, and he got drunk all the time, and he was having a great time up there, living the life of a king. And that should have been underlined a little bit more.

Gerry Lopez, who plays a Dayak, seems to be smiling all the time.

It's probably just him. He does have a wonderful presence, doesn't he? He looks like a King Dayak, and he's so agile. He learned all of their moves and could do them as well as they could. He could climb trees as fast as they could, he could run through the jungle, he could move totally without any noise. There's a wonderful sequence—they took it out 'cause it was pretty violent—where he shoots some Japanese and he's like a pointer. He's moving, and then we see him raise his carbine, and we go to the Japanese, they're moving and he can't see them, and then they go a little farther, and then he shoots them. They don't have a chance.

The touches of Conrad: a man not being able to escape his own past, always being drawn back into them—

— oh, I'm always influenced by Conrad—

— and by Lawrence of Arabia, as in the moment when Nigel Havers is going to kill the infant whose mother has died in childbirth. It's close to the moment when Lawrence executes Gassim, only Learoyd backs off and says to Havers, astonished, "You were going to kill him!"

— and Havers responds, equally astonished, "You were going to let me!"

Flight of the Intruder

Nat Segaloff: You're an uncredited writer on this film, which is about two hotshot Navy pilots (Willem Dafoe and Brad Johnson) who make an unauthorized bombing run on Hanoi during the Vietnam war—doing, in effect, what their own government refuses to do. Robert Dillon and David Shaber get screen credit.

John Milius: I wrote the whole script. That was one of my great fights with the Writers Guild; they struck my name from it because I was the director.

Was this because you weren't established as a collaborator from the beginning?[44]

No, it was that if you're a director—and, particularly, *me*—they weren't going to give you credit!.

If you rewrite more than 51 percent, you get credit, don't you?

Um-hmm. But I have a lot of enemies in the Writers Guild. Everybody agreed it was a dirty deal, but there is no appeal. Even David Shaber believed I should have had that first credit.

---

44 Briefly, WGA rules insist that, for a director to get writing credit, he must either be established as a collaborator from the beginning, or contribute more than 51 percent of a script. An arbitration hearing is automatic when someone's name is added to a script after the first draft.

The film is about professionals who do their job, even when their own superiors get in the way.

There are moments in war for compassion, for what could be called compassion. There are also moments for direct action, or what could be called clarity. For example, there's a letter Kurtz writes to his son in *Apocalypse Now* that Willard reads:

> In a war there are many moments for compassion and tender action. There are many moments for ruthless action—what is often called ruthless, but may, in many circumstances, be only clarity—seeing clearly what there is to be done, and doing it: directly, quickly, awake, looking at it.

That's my answer to that.

There's a character named Jack Barlow in Flight of the Intruder who's in the Navy, but the Jack Barlow in Big Wednesday goes into the Army.

That was some *other* Jack Barlow (smiles).

So much for intertextuality.

Rough Riders

Nat Segaloff: *When you make an historical film such as Rough Riders about Teddy Roosevelt and San Juan Hill do you have a responsibility to tell history accurately, even though it's a movie?*

John Milius: You can change the truth as long as you have the spirit of the truth. You can't tell the truth exactly all the time. Everybody has the right to interpret the truth. What do they say? History is just a lie that is accepted by everybody. Or Grant's definition of history which is "One God damned thing after another."[45]

History is written by the winners. When you sketch the character of Teddy Roosevelt as being very blustery, over-the-top, a man who is aware of his own legend at the same time he is living it, that's making a statement.

But he *was* that way. He enjoyed himself. I don't think he was aware of his own legend as much as he enjoyed himself. He had "the great enthusiasm" as he talks about. He was a victim of the great enthusiasms.

How do you direct an actor to give a performance that could be seen as out of step stylistically with the other characters?

---

[45] This quote is also attributed to Arnold Toynbee, Henry Ford, and Edna St. Vincent Millay.

I didn't have to do that. All I had to do was turn Tom Berenger—who is an historian and a stickler for detail as well as a matchless actor—loose and say, "Here's material on Teddy Roosevelt"—which he already had a considerable amount of, by the way. He himself went and got tapes so he could hear how he actually sounded. He got his eyeglasses from the same place that Roosevelt made his eyeglasses. He had five or six pairs with him at all times, the way Teddy did, some sewn into his hat, some onto his pockets. In the movie he gets a pair shot off from behind—the bullet goes past his eye and shoots the glasses off—and he reaches around and gets another pair. Teddy Roosevelt is an extraordinary character. He's almost a god. He's Alexander the great, an exceptional character for any time. If he were in Rome he would have been a match for Caesar.

Theodore Roosevelt appears throughout your films.

He is just a marvelous character. Everything that's good about America is exemplified in Teddy Roosevelt. There's something about him. He is a perfect hero because he's not always right. He's wonderfully flawed and over-zealous, and he's truly a character bigger than life. Did you ever hear about the time he was shot while giving a speech while running for president on the Bull Moose ticket? He had a book in his pocket and the book slowed the bullet but it penetrated his chest anyway. He was bleeding, and he fell back, and his hand [went up] and he continued his speech while they grabbed the assassin and brought him to him. He said, "Let me look into his face." And he looked into the face of this guy and said, "Pitiful! Take him away!" and continued his speech bleeding through his coat[46].

How did you become aware of him?

---

46 John Flammang Schrank shot TR with his .38 Colt police special on October 14, 1912 at a speech in Milwaukee, Wisconsin, later claiming at his trial that former President William McKinley had come to him in a dream and ordered the hit. Flammang died in 1947 in a mental hospital. TR died in 1919.

My father thought he was the greatest president we ever had, he could do everything. He was like Alexander the Great. He was a great, great writer, a great naturalist, a great outdoorsman, a great statesman, a great warrior, and a great thinker. He was very rich, but he always was in touch with the common man, and his heart was always totally with the common man. He was the first real populist president. If you look at his policies today they seem almost Communistic. But he was not one of these arrogant, wealthy, distant, privileged princes. He was truly a man of the people.

Could he have survived the late Twentieth Century?

I think so, because there are very few people of that magnitude. When you encounter characters like that in history, like Caesar, they are so obvious. Caesar, Gaius Marius, Roosevelt, Alexander—many, many characters like that, they stick right out. All these characters must be flawed. If they're too goody-goody they don't work any more.

Are you talking dramatically or historically?

Historically. They don't have any impact when they're wonderful and everything they do is great. It doesn't mean anything.

Did Tom Berenger look at The Wind and the Lion first to see how Brian Keith played Roosevelt?

He'd seen it and he really liked it, but he just did his research, and that's all he had to do. He was going to do it as accurately as he could, and he did it wonderfully. It's a more accurate Teddy Roosevelt than Brian Keith's was.

How did Brian Keith feel about being in Rough Riders, playing President McKinley opposite another actor playing the role he played 25 years earlier?

He just wanted to be in the movie so much. Teddy Roosevelt in *The Wind and the Lion* was his favorite thing that he ever did. He knew he was dying, and he wanted to do this; he probably wanted to die right on the set. He was as lucid and sharp as could be, but he didn't have much physical energy, and he didn't care. He told dirty jokes all day and had a wonderful time, and he probably said, "Well, I didn't die down there," and he went home and that's when he shot himself. He probably said, "Well, I've still got the glow of having done something that I really liked, and it's better if I go out this way." He never got his due, but he got to live the life, and he lived it well; he always had enough money and everything else. He was a really great actor and a very good man.

There were some changes in the structure of Rough Riders from the script—some of the opening sequences were switched around. Roosevelt's War College speech now comes after the attack on the Lusitania, rather than before, and so forth. When did that happen?

Probably on the editing table. We'd never thought of a title sequence, so we created one that told the politics.

It's a really well-done, romantic, muscular film where, for the first time, you understand what the Spanish-American war was about.

What I liked was that it's very even-handed about the war. It shows that maybe we didn't have the most noble motives for getting in the war.

That's not exactly a revelation.

But they bring it up and they talk about it. There's the scene before San Juan Hill when they say, "There's those who say we're just doing this to make the world safe for Wall Street."

And then one guys says, "I don't care; I'm here for the regiment." And Francesco Quinn (Rafael Castillo) stands up and makes that speech that's what all the propaganda has told us that war has always been about: "We're here for the little guy. When men with guns and boots come and take his food and his woman, he hopes that America will come and set things right."

There's a sense of ennui that suffuses the men after the battle, almost as if to say they'll never have it this good again.

To me that's the whole movie, in those moments. I always look for something that is not in any other film. I don't know if that kind of sequence is in any other film.

Most films end when the story is finished, before the characters fully react to what has happened. It takes a while to realize that the good days are over.

They're not "the good days are over" because you get your well-won reward. The characters in my movies don't go off with pots of money and live happily ever after. They're going to live the way the rest of us live. In a sense, nobody knows what they've done. To me, one of the most realistic characters in *Rough Riders* is Bardshar (Eric Allan Kramer). He goes back a hero, his wife is gone, the family store is empty, so he sits down lights a cigar. But you don't know whether he's going to live his life alone or go off and become a drunk. I always like to think that good comes to Bardshar.

When you're writing a 183-minute movie for television what do you have to learn or re-learn about script structure?

Well, you have to keep it going. You have to keep it exciting. I don't know; I just loved the idea of writing something longer.

Do you have to hew to commercial breaks?

No, I never pay attention to that. There's natural pauses.

How do you find classic weapons, like in Rough Riders, *the German machine gun?*

Most of it's still around. Places have them for rent. I remember we were doing a reshoot and I ordered some guns from Stembridge. I ordered a couple of pump shotguns. And, of course, as I'm leaving home to do second unit stuff north of Los Angeles, I thought I better grab my old .97 because they'll probably send just regular A-70 pump shotguns that were made in the 50s. And they did. So all of the close-ups of the shotgun are mine.

Did you account for all of them after the production?

Oh yeah. I don't have any interest in artillery. (Pause; smiles) I wouldn't mind a mortar...

Back to Writing for Hire

Nat Segaloff: *You wrote* Geronimo *and Walter Hill directed it. Did you undergo a quest so you could purify yourself first?*

John Milius: No, but I feel that, all the time, I was in touch with the spirit of the Bronco Apaches. If not Geronimo, certainly Magnus Coloradus! But I felt I was in touch with Geronimo; I felt I really knew this man. The American Indian is someone it's very easy for me to deal with. I could very easily be an Indian without any trouble.

Since you are a Mongologist, I'm trying to draw a continuum between Gengis Khan and Geronimo.

Well, they were all Mongols. They all had the same ancestry; they came from the same place, not very long ago by historical time. They say those people came down about the time of the Dark Ages, not even Christ. They had the same origins.

Your script of Geronimo *is very spiritual, it's very moving, and you can follow the story and know that the war starts when the tribe's Shaman is killed. In the movie you're, what, 45 minutes into it before that happens. You and Walter Hill have made a couple of films together —*

No, no, he's just taken my films and ruined them.

Extreme Prejudice *the same way.*

Yeah. *Extreme Prejudice* and *Geronimo*. The results are there to look at. God has his schedule and methods. I don't question them.

In Extreme Prejudice there's a nice Henry and Becket thing between Nick Nolte and Powers Boothe—enemies who used to be friends. I love it when two characters know each other so intimately that they predict each other's moves and it becomes a real mind game as well as an action game.

D'jever read the script? It's a lot different than that[47]. You could practically make *Extreme Prejudice* again right now because that film has so little to do with it. Now I'll give you an example of somebody who changed the script and made a good movie, and had me change a lot of the script, and had a lot of other people change it, too, and that's *Jeremiah Johnson*. Because Sydney Pollack is not stupid. Sydney Pollack is a very intelligent man, and he's a very skilled filmmaker. When we were making that movie he didn't particular like me. He thought I was crazy, he thought I was a maniac, and he was totally disturbed by me, I think, that he went to his analyst and talked about me all the time. But Sydney is an extremely intelligent and skilled director, and he made a movie which is not the movie I started out to make. I can't say that that movie is my original script. We all ended up there. Where we all ended up was a good place.

The film is nothing like your script. How does it twist you around when you write something—whether it's Geronimo or Texas Rangers—and you watch somebody else come in —

— and ruin it?

---

47 Milius's shooting script marked "Rev. 8-25-76" concerns a "black op" by U.S. Special Forces who illegally take over the small town of Uvalde to see how easily the government can institute Martial Law, despite the opposition of a diligent Texas Ranger. By the time it went into production, however, a completely unrelated subplot had been grafted on involving drug smuggling by an old buddy of the Texas Ranger.

Yeah.

Well, how do you think? It sure doesn't make you feel good, does it?

Can you write a script they can't fuck up?

They can fuck up anything, they can change anything. And they do, they change it and ruin it.

Why do they take a good script—a script that was good enough for them to buy it—and fuck it up?

Because they're *stupid*! They get the thing, and it's a good script, and then they get in the position of power, and they want to show off, so they decide that they know better how to make this movie. For whatever reason. For the reason of the director saying, "I have a vision of it" to the producer saying, "I know what'll make money." There are any number of excuses, but there's only one explanation: they're stupid. And the results show it.

You wrote Texas Rangers[48] for someone else to direct?

No, I wrote it for me.

And then they wouldn't let you do it?

They wouldn't let me. They never asked me. I was going to direct it years before. It's not even releasable. They may go straight to video. They were supposed to release it six months ago [mid 2000]. It's a piece of crap, and so it ain't gonna have my name on it and [have] people say, "How do you feel that it's a piece of crap?" Well, I feel awful that it's a piece of crap, but it's nothing that I had anything to do with. If they're gonna

---

48 The founding of the Texas Rangers was packaged as a *Young Guns* with badges.

be stupid and ruin something, ultimately, you can't do anything about it. I found [the rewritten script] mean-spirited and overly violent and nasty and phony. The script I took my name off of was totally inaccurate, nothing to do with history. I always remember the story of Cezanne and the apples. Cezanne was painting a still life with hills behind it in the inimitable Cezanne style, and someone said, "I don't like the apple." So he cut the apple out. He had a better attitude than we do, I guess.

Did the check clear?

Oh, the checks do clear. I was the most highly paid because they bought me off once before, then they had to buy me off again.

Martin Ritt always used to say that he makes the film the way it should be made, and if they're stupid enough to want to recut it, let 'em, it's their film. But I think that was disingenuous because I know he had passion for it.

I have enormous passion too. Like I say, I have great bitterness. But I think, like the gladiator (viz *Gladiator*), "in this life or the next I will have my revenge." But what can you do?

Let me ask you about **Clear and Present Danger**[49] *(Phillip Noyce, 1994). From a mechanical point of view, when you're confronted with a 500-plus page novel, how do you start adapting it?*

Those two—*Hunt for Red October* and *Clear and Present Danger*—were very easy to do because [Tom] Clancy is a blowhard and he loves to tell how much he knows about everything. So there really isn't a lot to change. the stories are pretty simple, and all you have to do is follow the story and not go into details

---

49 Tom Clancy's sprawling adventure in which Jack Ryan (Harrison Ford) discovers a drug smuggling operation being carried out with the knowledge of, if not direct orders from, the Oval Office.

on the cavetation of the propellers on submarines or how the FBI tracks a killer in this place or this young boy shoots him with a .22. There's a million sub-stories that were not attached to the main story. What the main story of *Clear and Present Danger* is, is not the drug lords, it's not the drugs, it is the opportunistic career-oriented people within politics in and the military in our society as careerists. It is the lack of a bigger morality.

How do you first encounter the material? Galleys, book, manuscript pages. . .?

That one was a book. It was a best-seller before they were going to make a movie of it.

Do you go through with a Magic Marker and highlight the sections that you think will make it into the movie?

Not really. I think I just went through and knew what should come next and what should come next.

Do you write it down as you go?

I stopped writing stuff down on pads a long time ago, although with that one, I think I did write down something just to keep track of scenes. I condensed a lot of it too; I went right to the thing to cut it down, get right to it.

Did they first send you the book and ask if you would you be interested in adapting it?

Yeah, I mean, I knew that book, and I said, "Sure."

Did you make a condensation the first time you read it?

No, the first time I read it, I just read it. I don't really work till I have to work. See, I believe a lot in the writing process, in having confidence in yourself and confidence in your abilities and leaving things up in the air. In other words, if you plan it all out, it's gonna be dead. So to keep it alive, I don't want to really know where I'm going tomorrow.

You weren't going to direct this, so you had to write it for someone else.

I just wanted to write it as a clear and concise screenplay. But I don't really know where I'm gonna go from day to day. I sorta know where the ending is gonna be. In something like *LeMay* (q.v.), I knew roughly that the third part, the final part, was gonna be the Cuban Missile Crisis, and I knew I would end it at his retirement. But I didn't know how I was gonna get there. There were a lot of scenes I had thought of a long, long time ago that I threw away in the process of getting ready to write.

Do you think in terms of what kind of scenes are going to make people put money into the film, scenes that will play on the screen—three good scenes, as they say, will sell a script.

I just have to find the scenes very interesting, something that has a natural dramatic tension, real dramaturgy to it. I have no idea what somebody else is going to think.

What are the hardest kind of scenes for you to write?

I don't think any scenes as being hard. If I have to write a boring scene—where you have to think of a way to get from here to there—I try and find a new way to do it. I regard that as a challenge, and I try to find some approach to make that interesting. Doing an action scene is interesting.

These days when they want to cut character scenes out of films and make them all action, how do you establish character in a very short, concise way?

You have to make people memorable. You have to make them do things that are memorable and real and have a certain impact. It's hard to say how you develop characters. You either do it or you don't; I really think it comes down to whether you have a knack for it or you don't. You try and make people quirky and interesting.

Else why would we want to spend two hours with them?

Yeah. If you have a hero and the hero is able to prevail all the time, he's not very interesting. If you have a hero who's a Viking and he kills everybody he comes up against because he's such a great swordsman or axe man, if he gets into a fight with the king's champion, we don't really care, because he's been able to dispatch hoards of other people, so he's going to be able to dispatch this guy. But if we're not sure—is he going to be able to dispatch this guy? What advantage he can get, or what luck? Or maybe he's not as good. That's more interesting. I like people who take risks, who think of themselves as something bigger. What I dislike about actors in general is what George Bernard Shaw said, that an actress is something more than a woman and an actor is something less than a man. The reason for that is that most actors think that they're the center of the universe, and therefore they're boring, because what kind of a universe is it if you're the center of it? A true hero is never the center of the universe. The true hero is someone who realizes that there is something bigger than he, and achieves a certain dignity by giving himself to that.

Your villains, too—with the possible exception of Thulsa Doom—are as complex as the heroes and have flaws.

They have to be real. If you look at the most villainous people, they always have a story. Look at it from their side. Did the Nazis get up every day and say, "I'm going to be a good Nazi today so I've got to get myself in a fiend mode? I've got to sit down and think of how I'm going to round up more Jews, how I can shoot more prisoners. How I can do things like that so I can be a good Nazi?" No. They think they're right when they're doing these things. You have to get into their minds.

That's why I don't like James Bond movies. All I can think of is the villain going in front of the local zoning board to get a variance in order to build his mountaintop fortress.

The best commentary on that is Austin Powers where the villain is this wonderful Dr. Evil who is much more interesting than Austin Powers. He gets up every day to be this great villain, and he has all this stuff, and he has problems, his son doesn't understand him. I don't know if they can make a third movie[50]; they've used up Austin Powers—we've heard all his jokes. The next one will have to be called "Dr. Evil" because he's the best character.

You're only as good as your enemy.

The other thing that's nice about villains is that you can pull out all the stops. You can have them say wonderful things. But they always have to have a point of view. Like John Dillinger saying, "You'd do what I do if you had the nerve."

Steve Zaillian and Donald Stewart are also credited on Clear and Present Danger. Was this one of those where they brought it around to everybody?

I wrote the first draft and wrote the sequence where they ambush the Suburbans (SUVs), and Steve Zaillian added a sequence where they're dueling back and forth with computers. Everybody added something to it. Steve Zaillian and I had a wonderful ending that they never used, which is too bad. The character of Cortes, the drug kingpin (Joachim de Almeida)

---

50 Nevertheless, they made *Goldmember* (2002)

was a good character, and we had this whole other ending how he goes to Washington to kill off the National Security Advisor (Harris Yulin), who is the real villain, while he's jogging in Washington. In fleeing afterwards, Cortes runs through a bad neighborhood and is accosted by thugs who say, "You've got to give us your money, man, because we need our dope!" They shoot him, but he manages to kill the guy who wounds him fatally. Before he lumbers off to die, the dope addict says, "You don't understand, man. I understand where you're coming from, but I need my dope." It's one of his customers who's done him in! And Cortes sits on a bench in the Mall looking at the Capitol all night, and as the sun is coming up, it's dawn, and he takes out and lights up a Cuban cigar—because it's illegal—and smokes it and laughs hysterically, looking at the Capitol, and he dies. But we couldn't use it because Harrison Ford didn't have a scene that good. And it's a terrible ending now where Harrison says, "I'm gonna go to the Senate and testify in closed session." Well, we know the Senators are just as rotten as the President! How is he gonna expose this before the Senate? They exposed everything about Waco, and it did a hell of a lot of good, didn't it? What good is the Senate gonna do? So I had him [Harrison Ford as Jack Ryan] go in and blackmail the President. He goes in there and the President asks him if he wants a job and he says, "No, I want to expose all this. I want my job as the Deputy Director of the CIA, but the only way is that I want something from you for the rest of your term, otherwise I am gonna expose you." The President says, "What's that?" Ryan says, "Honor." "You have no right to talk to me this way; I'm the President of the United States!" He says, "Is it a deal?" "Okay, it's a deal." That's a much better ending!

Alec Baldwin, who played Jack Ryan in **Red October***, is much closer to the character that Tom Clancy created than Harrison Ford. How do you get past the fact that Han Solo/Indiana Jones is playing someone who's basically a paper-pusher?*

They get him hanging off the skids of helicopters shooting machine guns.

Changing the Way Scripts are Written

Nat Segaloff: Why do so many of your films use voice-over narration?

John Milius: Nothing's as good as somebody telling you a story. I'm not a pure filmmaker. I'm not an MTV guy. I go back to a much older technique. I really should be a novelist. I'm not fascinated with "film" and "movies." I watch film for stories, not the juxtaposition of image and graphics. I don't give a damn about equipment and lights, it's just a method of getting to the images. I'd just as soon have no special effects. So my whole concept of what I do goes back to the old thing of telling the story, of the Homeric ethic of being able to tell the tale of the Trojan wars again and again until finally it's written down by somebody, and nobody knows who Homer was.

It also provides a closure, a sense of hope, given that the narrator has lived through the tale in order to tell us the story.

You feel it really happened and really mattered in somebody's life that it got passed down by the tribe to you.

I wonder if, in cultures where there is more leisure time and things move more slowly, people are more inclined to develop an oral tradition.

When I was making *Dillinger*, I met farmers we would rent stuff from, and they were extremely witty. We would shoot on a farmer's place that had a great old shack that looked like something out of the 30s. The guy had bib overalls—of course, they were all millionaires but they didn't live like it—and they were all extremely witty and sharp in a laid-back, Midwestern farmer way. You could never get the last word. They were very intelligent and very careful and very good joke and story tellers. I said, "Why are you so fast, it's pretty hard to get around you?' And they said, "Well, wheat takes a long time to grow."

Your scripts for The Life and Times of Judge Roy Bean, Dillinger and The Wind and the Lion are written in the past tense. They say you're not supposed to do that, that film is always in time-present because it happens as we watch.

I wanted to do something different. When I wrote *Roy Bean* I wanted to write it better than it needed to be. I didn't like the way screenplays were written. Matter of fact, I give myself full credit that the form today is my form, eliminating "cut to" and a lot of stuff like that. Describing settings. Like *The Wind and the Lion* opens "A gull screams" and then you go right into it, you open on the image. Or "The Desert—Caravan to Fez." You don't cut to "close shot—desert—caravan to Fez." It's just what it is. With *Rough Riders* it's "Sagamore Hill, Oyster Bay." That's all you need to know; you don't need to know what kind of shot it is.

Do you write differently for yourself to direct as opposed for somebody else?

I write the same all the time.

Some of your scripts, you almost direct them on paper.

But I never sit there and violate my own rules. I never say, "We see such-and-such." I've opened up somebody's script and it'll say, "We see so-and-so. He is a handsome man of 28, tall and powerful nature. He is the type of man who would do such-and-such." How do we *know* he's a handsome man? How do we *know* how old he is? How do we *know* what kind of things he would do? You have to *learn* it through the *dialogue* and what he *does*! Or "we track with the camera down the hall." *Why are we tracking?* If you can't do it better than that—if you can't describe how we get down the hall better than "we track with the camera"—you aren't much of a writer.

Are scripts written for filmmakers, or are they written for some production executive who may not know a dolly shot from a crane shot?

I don't think they should have ever had dolly shots and crane shots. I write my scripts so they're novelistic and tell a story. I hated the form of screenplays and I wanted to develop a simpler form that was more in line with telling a story and, I must say, it's in line with the forms that scripts are written today.

What was the first film you saw where you were aware that films are written?

Probably *Red River* (Howard Hawks, 1948). I watched it with a friend and after it was over he turned to me and said, "People don't really talk like that, but ya wish they did."

Let's get into the actual script process. Syd Field, John Truby, Linda Seger and others have written how-to books, and now everybody thinks that something has to happen on page nine, something turns on page 60, and so forth. What do you think about this?

Syd Field doesn't write successful screenplays. Ultimately that's a bunch of hogwash. There are screenplays that I have written that are going to be around a lot longer than his book.

But you're up against it when some kid production executive has taken one course and thinks he knows everything about screenplays.

Then you're out of luck. Your time is over and they make those kind of movies. But you have to be true to your art. You have to be true to your style. This isn't a game. It has to be real, with real people and a real story, real incident and real drama. It can't be "We're gonna put so many pieces from column A and so many pieces from column B." Even though that works and makes people a living, it doesn't make for a real lasting piece of work.

Audiences seem to pay their ticket money anyway.

Audiences will go to the movies. They're obsessed with celebrities in the movies. They'll pay to see *any* movie. They're not going to see these movies 'cause they're good movies; they'll even *tell* you they're lousy movies.

But they still go to them.

They go to them, yeah, because it's the thing to do.

What screenwriters have influenced you?

The only one that influenced me—somewhat, about dialogue—was Robert Bolt. There was a kind of flair, a cynicism. He was always writing *about* something. He and I got on very well, which you wouldn't think because of our politics[51]. A year

---

51 Bolt was a fervent anti-war activist and once had to be bailed out of jail by producer Sam Spiegel during the shooting of *Lawrence of Arabia*.

before he died he wrote me a letter and told me he was writing a book, saying, "And they leave you alone!" He liked my films; he loved *The Wind and the Lion, Farewell to the King,* and *Big Wednesday.*

Can the audience be programmed to know, for example, that a prop that's introduced in the first five minutes of a film is going to save the day in the last fifteen minutes, or that a minor character who is given a name early in the film will be exposed as the villain at the end, or —

Nah, that has nothing to do with it. It's just bad, like high school. High school culture has encompassed everything. Everybody goes and does things because it's "hip" or "cool" or whatever. People are more like lemmings than they've ever been, and they're encouraged to be like lemmings. Everybody wants to be "in the know" or *au courant,* so they follow the pack. It's a virtue today to be "ahead of the curve" or "cutting edge." There is no virtue any more in great skill or a mastery of something. Advertisers and media people sell this. If that's all kids hear while they grow up, that's going to become the virtues they have—not the virtue of steadiness of honor or loyalty or honesty. They're not going to have the virtues of great skill or excellence; they're going to have the virtues of being hip. And it's a wonderful thing to sell hipness, because you can change it all the time and sell more of it.

Your films have a notable lack of hipness. I don't mean they're stodgy, I mean that they don't contain slang, for example. Your dialogue is true but not necessarily current.

I try and make the dialogue as much like the period as possible. If it's *Rough Riders* they're going to talk the way they talked in 1898. If it's *Clear and Present Danger* they're going to talk the way they talked when that takes place. When I do *Flight of the Intruder* they use a lot of hippie terms. When Willem Dafoe is asked, "What do you think of bombing Hanoi," he doesn't say, "I think it's a good idea," he says, "Cool, man." That's all you can do—make them talk like people talk when the movie took place.

In Big Wednesday *you have them use the word* radical *quite a bit.*

It's a surfer film. I never tried to teach the audience the correct surfer language and I never tried to tell them what it meant. You didn't have to know what a cutback was. If a guy says, "He's got a really boss cutback," that's all you need to know.

Do you say your lines out loud?

No. I just write them.

Do you laugh at funny stuff?

Sometimes. When it's outrageous or I think of a good one. You start getting in the spirit of something and you just get in the mood.

Have you ever had a character just pop into your script and you can't get rid of him?

Oh, you can always get rid of them, but sometimes characters do materialize and become more than you expect.

They say that if you can switch two scenes in a script, they're both in the wrong place.

I don't have any rules. I just do whatever I want. I usually have my scenes in the right order—although I did switch some things around in *LeMay* to make things clearer in the second draft. There was a Sergeant character who was in a ball turret and he tried to bail out over Schweinfurt. The plane was on fire and he was given permission to bail out right over the target. They dropped their bombs and he was gonna burn to death, so he was going to pull some explosive bolts and open the ball turret and just fall out the back of it. Well, in doing it, he somehow pulled his ripcord and the turret was turned around and air rushed in and blew his parachute open. He got out, but the parachute wrapped around his feet, jammed up against the guns. So he's hanging upside down out the bottom of the ball turret on the bottom of the B-17, which is turning off the target and heading toward the Alps. In the recounting I read of the battle, one of the pilots made a comment about "a strange object hanging off the bottom of a B-17 at nine o'clock." Well, in fact, it was this guy, and he lived because he was finally able to get his feet to hit the electrical button to turn the turret around, and then the wind blew against his back so he just did a sit-up into the turret because the wind was with him then. The plane flew through a cloud and put the fires out. So he survived the battle and survived the war. Then there was another incident that I knew was true, at the end of the story, that, at the very height of the Cuban missile crisis, there were secret squadrons of B-52s circling over the Canadian border. Everybody was at Def-Con 3, which means that it's no drill, it's war. A general was in charge of an air defense base in upper Michigan, right on the border—his planes are loaded with nuclear-tipped missiles and his pilots are sitting there, ready to go to war, this is going to be it. If the bell rings, it can't be anything but that the Russians are here or they're trying to sabotage us, and the thing is started, and these F-106s are going to go up and shoot whatever's coming in. And, in fact, a bear had torn down the fence and set off all the claxons at Def-Con 3. What this General really did was to have somebody drive his car across the runway, and he had to talk the pilots in these F-106s out of taking off. Those that had taken off, he had to talk into coming back, because if they cleared the clouds and saw what was there, they would have seen these secret B-52s and thought they were Russians, and they would have shot their nuclear-tipped missiles at them and the war would have started and the whole world would have come to an end. That's how close we came; that's the closest point in the Cuban Missile Crisis, *and it's not even talked about!* They talk about the Kennedys and all this stuff, but that was the closest point. *A grizzly bear brought us to the brink of destruction!* So I decided to have this character who was hanging out of the turret over Schweinfurt go throughout the whole movie as one of LeMay's men. He becomes a radio operator over Japan, he becomes an officer during the Berlin Airlift, and he becomes, at the end, the General in charge of this base. Because the idea of a guy hanging upside down over Schweinfurt and surviving—God had to decide that *this* guy must save the world at the end. You don't do that by cards. When I knew those two incidents—I don't know if I decided it then or whatever—but when I wrote the incident of the guy hanging out of the turret, I knew this guy *had* to save the world.

When you're doing an original script, how much thinking or planning do you have to do before you actually sit down and start writing?

Well, you gotta do as much research as you can to make it real, and you gotta know sorta where you're going, then you don't wanna do too much planning, because if you do too much planning, it'll become dull. And I think that's what most writers do, and why most screenplays are so dull.

All the beat sheets, every step outline, every treatment—and then there's nothing left?

The same thing with executives who write down how they're gonna fix it, and they all put in their two bits. How can the thing have any life of its own?

Look at it the other way: you take a well-planned script to the set. You have perfected that script over two or three years. But then somebody makes an ad-lib that sounds better, only it really isn't better, it's just new, and you're bored with your script, so you put it in.

When I go to the set to direct a movie, it's all up for grabs. The actors are in awe of the script because they know I'm a famous writer, so they're always a little wary of wanting to change anything. So *I* often change things. If an actor has a problem and comes up to me, unless it's something I really need for exposition later, I'll always change it for him, I'll change it three or four times. I have no problem with that. On *Rough Riders* we lost a day because the [dailies were] sabotaged, but they wouldn't give us the day back; they said, "We've got to cut the battle in the jungle way down."

   I said, "Okay, I won't be able to have the detail of following these three columns the way I wanted to, so I'm going to somehow cut down the detail and move them up and make that up as I go."
   Well, it drove the script girl nuts. She said, "What happens when—?"
   I said, "Just write down what I do. It's all gonna work out later."
   "Well, I don't think this is gonna work out because I don't see a place where this is gonna come out. Scene such-and-such isn't there any more."
   I said, "Don't worry, I wrote it the first time, I can write it this time." And it's very clear in the movie. All three columns come out of the jungle at the same time as G Troop turns the flank, and then they charge and take the river. It's all right there. I knew exactly what I was doing, but I didn't know from moment to moment, I just knew where I was going, and what pieces I needed to get there.

They're always trying to remove the risks in this business.

Yeah, and having script writing classes in which people are actually trying to figure out formulas is insane.

A lot of people make money at it.

People can figure out how to make money out of anything.

A lot of the executives right outside this building would give anything to make it into a formula.

I think they're getting rid of a lot of those executives. Slowly.

Do people who approve movies even like movies?

They all come out of Development, whatever that means. Each one is worse than the one before him, and each one is interested in how, when they finally get into their position, even though they've participated in the stabbing of the guy who was there before, and watched two or three before that, as soon as one of these little liberal do-gooders get into the position of power, of course, it's the Thousand Year Reich.

The Value of Film

Nat Segaloff: Is film merely a storytelling medium or does it hold a higher artistic place in our culture?

John Milius: [Historical tales] tell the stories of valor and heroes and great enterprise that underline the better nature of men. And I think that's a worthwhile thing to do. Like in *Rough Riders*. You get something back. You're serving God, in essence, by doing that. You're not serving anything by just doing another episode of *Die Hard* or *Jurassic Park*.

The artist enriches people who have contact with his work. He builds something.

That's what I do. I build monuments. That's what my purpose is. I'm here to build monuments to the Rough Riders and to the Marines at Iwo Jima and the Son Tay raiders and, hopefully, Curtis LeMay.

But you're not doing it in bronze, you're doing it in the living medium of film where, every time it's shown, it brings people into time present.

I look at something like *Rough Riders* as a monument. It's like the Vietnam monument. There is no more powerful monument than the Vietnam Wall. That's a noble reason to make a film— to monumentalize something, to bring it to attention. Those things need to be built. You're not doing it for yourself or your glory or to make tons of money. *Big Wednesday*, there's a larger purpose there. It's a film about friendship. The greatest thing that I derived from surfing—other than the days of high adventure—was friendship. As far as movies go, I have no idea what's going to make tons of money; I have no more idea than you do or that guy out there [indicating the Warner Bros. executive offices] does. I don't think anybody does. Only Steven Spielberg does, and he's not even right all the time. If it was all about making money, we'd be making worse films than we do. It would be consistent; like making corn flakes. Now that's how a lot of people approach the business, but if you want to make good films you have to satisfy yourself.

What qualifies as a "good" film?

We don't know what movies are going to be considered the most important. A movie that was very important to me when I was growing up, and when I was in cinema school, and still go back and dip into, is *The Battle of Algiers* (Gillo Pontecorvo, 1965), which almost no one has seen. It's a great movie, as great today as when it was made, but it's never on television and a whole generation has grown up without seeing it.

And yet it influenced the New Wave and everybody else.

It's a ground-breaking film. Another series that was terribly important to me, that people have seen but don't take very seriously, are the Sergio Leone films. They look down their nose at Sergio Leone: "Oh, yes, spaghetti westerns." They're incredibly cynical, so they fit the era. There's things like that that you have to look at, and history has a strange way of viewing them. *Apocalypse Now* is a tremendously important film right now, but when it was up for an Academy Award® it was soundly beaten by *Kramer vs. Kramer* (Robert Benton, 1976). That night, all of Hollywood felt *Kramer vs. Kramer* was a far more worthy film than *Apocalypse Now*. I knew I wasn't gonna win anything when I went that evening. But twenty years from now, I suppose *Apocalypse* will still be an important film, but maybe *Kramer vs. Kramer* will be an important film again, too. Maybe it won't. Because there are films that are very important today that were taken with a grain of salt in their time. You don't know what's going to be a legend.

Most people insist that "any film that makes money is a good film."

That's bullshit. Many of the movies that we regard as great movies from the 40s or 50s, you don't even know how much money they made, or if they made any money at all. *It's a Wonderful Life* (Frank Capra, 1946) was such a great financial failure that it sunk Liberty Films. We don't know. We don't sit there and say this was a big hit in 1954 or something like that. History doesn't give a shit.

And yet Hollywood exists to make money.

It's a weird thing, but in trying to make money, they will occasionally make art. Or they'll make something that is lasting. Whatever it is, it's the same thing that Homer was trying to do.

When Homer was telling stories, he wasn't thinking whether he could make it into a ride at Aesopland. He wasn't thinking if he could make a board game.

Or an Achilles action figure.

When a movie is based on a book, after a while, people often forget that the book exists.

What you're given in a movie is never as good as what a novel gives you. In a movie you're given an image, the actor, the color of the sky; it's only that. In a film, it's all laid out there for you;

in a novel you have to provide it yourself. What makes film magic is the juxtaposition of these images, and the juxtaposition against music and movement and all the things Kubrick talks about as being pure film. There's an emotional moment in *Road Warrior* (George Miller, 1981) when you look out and you see these guys riding from the camp and they've captured two characters, they've got them up on the motorcycles and they're torturing them, and the Great Humongous is howling *in German!* And there's smoke and dust and it has nothing to do with storytelling, it's a pure visual moment that makes me want to stand up and howl like a wolf. *It has nothing to do with the movie!* Yes, it shows that they're barbarians, but somehow it does a wonderful thing: it makes you love the Barbarians and barbarity. That's where film has its power. It doesn't necessarily have its power in giving you the best interpretation of something; a novel does that because it uses your own mind. You have to think about what that street looks like when Ishmael says, "It's all that I can do to stop from knocking people's hats off, this dark, dank November in my soul." And you know what New Bedford looks like. When you meet Queequeg, no Queequeg can be as good as the Queequeg in the book. So *Moby Dick* can never really be done as a film; no *Moby Dick* is as good as the book. I had to change *Heart of Darkness* severely and increase its horsepower tremendously to make something that would equal the book, and I think I roundly succeeded, but only by upping the ante tremendously. But the visual ante is so much higher than the book. [In a film] You can't come upon a pile of elephant bones and say, "I feel Kurtz, he is near." It's not going to be the same thing as finding the tail of a B-52 stuck in a swamp and seeing a helicopter burning in a tree and say, "I feel Kurtz, he is near."

The baseline is always kicked up when you have a war going on.

The power of *Heart of Darkness* is so great that it requires it. That's why, when somebody tells a story that's really powerful, it has an indelible effect on me. In every one of my movies I have a scene—and I'll often cut it out—where somebody tells a really powerful story. It's just them talking. I can think of other movies where that's effective: Patton's speech is much more effective because *he's* telling it to you: "We're going to go through those lousy Hun bastards like crap through a goose." You are suddenly one of those guys in his tank corps ready to go over there. Another great scene is in the Bergman film *Persona*. Two women on the beach tell a story of an erotic encounter, a sexual incident. I don't even remember what the sexual incident was—I haven't seen the movie since I was very young—but I remember it was incredibly arousing to hear them talk about while they were laying there on the beach. There wasn't anything you saw except them, but you used your imagination, and so it was incredibly powerful.

Hollywood Hell

Nat Segaloff: Why is it so hard to get good movies made?

John Milius: We're in a time when people are specifically trying to do [movies] that are not about anything. We live in a time of enormous permissiveness, flagging morality—of *any* kind, not morality as sex—morality as business ethics. *Any* kind of morality. Even the Christian religious groups are turning on each other and running off and doing all these things. These are times when no one's sure of *anything*, so rather than deal with anything, it's best to make it about *nothing*. And *that's* where you have the Rambo concept: the hero that's just strong because you can count on strength.

There's so much money in movies, but it all seems like it's being earned by the same people, and everybody else in this town just wastes your time.

It's like the mountain men. The mountain men got rich from beaver hats and they made all this money, they had the beaver and people would meet them at rendezvous and sell the beaver hats and get thousands and thousands of dollars, and they took the money and did they go to St. Louis and buy estates? No. They bought a new horse. They could only have three horses if they were one person: a mule and two horses and what you could put on those three horses. You could put enough food for a month. You could put enough lead for a year. You could put enough powder for a year. Some beads, traps, clothing, things like that. You can fill up a horse pretty quick. Now at the end of that, you ain't spent your thousands of dollars. Now you buy the prettiest squaws. Pretty soon you're spent; you haven't got any more sperm; you've fucked yourself to a dither. Now you drink. You buy a keg. One keg would finish you. So at the end when everybody's picking up and leaving after a week on the Green River, this guy's got a pile of money. And what does he do? He burns it in the fire because he ain't gonna put it on that horse, because every ounce that goes on that horse is more important than money. But these guys had the choice every time. They made as much as $20,000 in one year. They could have given it to some guy to take back and put in the bank; I'm sure there are guys who offered to do that (laughs). Twenty thousand dollars! Do you know how much twenty thousand dollars was in 1828? I'm sure you could buy a nice home and a wife in St. Louis and have a bar and a whorehouse so you could cater to all your whims, and probably be quite prosperous. Some of 'em did. But the majority of 'em burned the money and got on the horse and rode off and returned to being a mountain man. Because if you're a mountain man, you *liked* being a mountain man.

As Spencer Tracy said about them in the narration at the beginning of How the West Was Won, "They wanted nothing beyond what they saw, and little of that."

"They wanted nothing beyond what they saw, and little of that." See, we've developed into a society that tells you that's totally wrong. It's interesting, because they were the first American entrepreneurs. I was looking at an ad for a Palm Pilot and it said, "This connects you to important Internet sites you will need, like TheStreet.com." And they showed this slick guy and he's got a suit on and a girl behind him, and this is who you want to be. It's hip and it's admirable and it's so fucking cutting-edge, and you can say such-and-such, 'Buy!' and while you're at it such-and-such, 'Sell!'" And I realized that this man—who's portrayed as an American hero, someone you want to grow up to be if you're a kid—ain't doing anything. He's buying and selling. He's just a professional Vegas gambler. He's going according to trends, and he's buying other people's production. He isn't producing anything.

We're a service economy. We raise people to work at McDonald's and to buy and sell other people's futures. We don't do anything.

He isn't taking his money and investing it in a company that is actually producing something: sun glasses, or cigars or bottles of water. He is just living off of managing the money that other people who produce these things are doing. And yet he is the new American hero. That's a far cry from the mountain men.

His hands are clean but his soul is dirty.

It isn't even that his soul is dirty. There *isn't* any soul.

When you make money it's because somebody pays you for something that didn't exist before you created it.

That's right. It's tangible. But the other thing is that if you do a service—if you're a fighter pilot—you're being paid to fly an aircraft and shoot at other airplanes and risk being shot down yourself. You're actually doing something that's extraordinary. If you're a doctor, you are doing something that's extraordinary; you are diagnosing people, telling them what's wrong with them, and offering to cure them and minister to them. That's a real thing.

How do you see yourself in the history of film and the commerce of this town?

I just try and make my monuments. I don't think I have a very big place—in fact, I have a very small place in the commerce of this town. I'm an anomaly. As far as the history goes, I'm always amazed that any of us has *any* place in film history. I mean, you tell me I do. You tell me I wrote all these great things and other people tell me I did, and I suppose it becomes history some day. Time will dignify anything. But when somebody says I'm a legend, I always say, "Well, if I'm a legend, what were the guys who were the *real* legends before us? The guys before us. Those guys really *did* stuff." I look at other people's stuff and they stand up there with anything. There's nothing [of mine] I could really look at and say, "That was a piece of shit." So I'm sorta proud of that. But I don't know how important any of this is really going to be in the light of history. History has a strange way of picking people out and making them more important than people you think are going to be important.

You of all people have a sense of history.

There are people who point it in their direction, but there are also people who get it changed. There are people who wanted to have enormous import and power or were very important at the time like General Nelson Miles, who really won the west. He won all the campaigns and wanted to be Chief of Staff, he wanted to take the Army to France in World War One, and he wanted to be president. But unless you're a historian you don't know who Nelson Miles was. Everybody sort of has heard of "Black" Jack Pershing who spent most of his years as a captain, and then became General of the Army with stars, a rank that's never been bestowed on anybody. Look at Douglas MacArthur: he knew the game he was playing, which is the way he was. He was aware all the time of who he was and the celebrity and the power. He was Caesar. That's really what he was. Naming that book *American Caesar* was the logical conclusion. There are so many similarities between him and Julius Caesar, it's amazing. He probably should have become the first Emperor of the United States.

He tried.

If he'd pulled it off, we'd be much better off today. He actually had a much better grasp of the concepts on which this country was founded than any politician since. We'd probably be a much freer country today with Emperor Douglas running things for a while. But today MacArthur is not as important in people's minds as Patton, who was a field general, a guy commanding an army, but one of three armies advancing under Eisenhower. Yet when people think of "the general" in World War Two, they think of Patton, and then they might think of MacArthur, and then maybe Eisenhower.

Why do you think that is?

Because there was a good movie made about him! That's how it works. He was lucky; he had Francis Coppola and George C. Scott.[52]

The artist has the ability to make sense out of his and other people's existences, too.

Is it sense, or is it just a story?

Why don't you tell me?

I don't know. It perplexes me a great deal. Morality can be changed and judged. There seem to be no absolutes any more. We're in a time where perception is everything, not whether it's real or not. Many times I've been in interviews and people

---

[52] *Patton* (Franklin J. Schaffner, 1970) was written by Edmund H. North and Francis Ford Coppola, who won Oscars® for adapted screenplay. George C. Scott played Patton and famously rejected his Oscar.®

have said, "You don't really do all this stuff that they say you do; you don't go hunting and shooting and hang out and smoke cigars with your friends and do all this macho old man, redneck shit that you say you do, do you? " People actually say that to me. I say, "I can't help it. I do all that stuff 'cause that's what I really like to do. I don't really give much of a damn about a lot of other things, and what I care about really is not that popular and I really don't care about what other people do." They say, "No, that's all an affected persona."

Why don't they want to believe that you are as you are?

Because people are not as *they* are.

And you are?

I'm not very good at hiding anything.

The notion of a guy making a movie with lots of millions of dollars—and, presumably, the whole mechanism of the studio behind him, having people listen to him for however many weeks it goes on—is a pretty powerful thing.

Oh, it's the *most* powerful thing. Everybody wants to direct. Why do they want to direct? Just that: so they can *direct*, so they can tell other people what to do. That's what really gets them off: to have all these people whirling about saying, "Tell me what to do." They can tell people what to do, they can judge them, they can be cruel, they can do all this stuff that they couldn't do in normal life. They can get away with murder. I mean, just look at the outfits they wear. To be a director, you have to wear a fucking baseball hat. Basically, they're trying to look like Steven Spielberg.

The really influential ones don't give a shit, they just make the movie.

Yeah.

Why do most people want to direct, and not write?

Nobody like to write because writing requires facing a blank page, which is not pleasant. Facing the blank page and coming up with good work is not easy to do.

How hard are you on what you write?

Extremely. As hard as I can be.

How do you know what's good and what isn't good?

When I'm excited by it and can't stop writing, then it's good. When I find it to be maudlin or predictable, I know it's bad.

How do you get to the zone of being able to write good stuff?

Boy, if I could tell you that, I could make a lot of money.

Do you have a ritual?

I used to dance with rattlesnakes.

And then they took over the studios, so you had to find another partner.

Yep. It's been a hard life because I have not had the comfort of drugs or drink like other writers.

Have you ever been blocked?

Yeah, many times. I'm blocked right now, today.

How do you unblock?

I hope something will happen. Sometimes you just get so guilty that you sit down and write. Right now I'm struggling to get started. Once I get started, I'm usually okay.

Do you remember the first time that you were truly pleased with something you wrote?

When I was 15 years old. I think it was an Indian story. Indians and mounted men or something. When I was in college I wrote some short stories that were very good and I was really exhilarated by those, and I read 'em not too long ago and they were still pretty good.

You saved all your stuff?

I don't have all of 'em. There was a series of stories I did when I was going to college and I was a lifeguard, and I wrote about surfing and a bunch of characters who were surfing and going through much the same thing. It was very much in a Steinbeck mode.

Most teenagers hate writing. They won't even write thank-you notes to Santa Claus. And here you are writing fiction.

Yeah, but I didn't like writing either. It was work.

But you did it. You felt compelled to do it.

I remember there were certain things I was quite proud of when I realized I knew how to write. I could write stories in different styles and things like that. I wrote an essay on *Moby Dick*, and it was really good; I wish I had it.

Did you ever get any of your prose pieces published?

Yeah, but in minor things.

Anything in surfing magazines or adventure magazines?

No, no. I never tried that. When I went to USC I wrote stuff for magazines, articles and things like that, and then Willard Huyck and I would write porno magazines. We'd have to do the whole thing in 24 hours.

This was for a fee?

Cheap porno magazines. They'd give us spaces where writing was to go.

So you'd give them—pardon the expression—eight inches.

You could just make up whatever stories you wanted, in any style. But I was able to call myself a professional.

What do you think your ratio is to what you write and throw away to what you write and keep?

Pretty close. Closer than most people. I don't know what the ratio is, but once it gets down and gets written, it doesn't get fooled with that much. Later I go back and cut things. But I'm not one to tend to go back. If the writing's going good, I don't go back and re-do it.

When you're writing something entirely on your own, as opposed to adapting a book, do you a treatment first, a beat sheet, or start right in on the blank page?

I just write on the blank page.

"Fade in."

Yeah. That other stuff just doesn't work. It makes for dull. Procedures, you know?

How scary is that?

That's the scariest thing there is.

Do you have to have X percent of the story in your head before you start writing it?

It's like you've got a jigsaw puzzle that's gonna fill the whole table, and you've got millions of little pieces that you can put together, and you don't know where it's gonna go, and you put this together, and you put a corner together, and finally you get enough on there that it starts to resemble a shape. And finally the shape has whatever the picture is gonna be.

Do you scroll back and forth and rewrite sections of your script?

No, not at all. Sometimes I'll go back and fix something or remember to go back and fix it later when I'm done, but I like to get through to the end.

Do you go back and make sure names are consistent and tidy up?

Yeah, but I'm not so concerned with that. Once you're writing it takes on a certain organic nature, and to interfere with that is very bad. When writing is good you really don't know what the people are gonna do each day. They surprise you because they're alive. If you go back and fix things, you're being much too manipulative. You have much too much control. You don't want to have that kind of control over it. You want to have the thing a little bit out of your control.

Let's take Farewell to the King *as an example of a script with lots of grays in it in an age when everybody wants black and white. How do you deal with this need for absolute right and absolute wrong in movies?*

You deal with any kind of disagreement by fighting. By struggle. Ultimately you have to say how much you are willing to put in. Are you willing to get fired over having it your way? As John Huston said, there is a time when you have to take that long walk down the road. There's also a point where you say, "If I change this, it won't really compromise what I intend to do, and it will get it made. It may be something I liked, but I'll lose that because it's more important for the thing to get made *and* it can still be what it is. It is *not* more important for it to get made and *not* be what it is.

How much you can change before you realize you've compromised?

You know what's right and wrong. You know when it's no longer what you wanted to write about, when it's not the story you wanted to tell. Now, you can be very prissy about the whole thing and throw fits and pretend you're a prima donna and everything should be done your way—Thomas Jefferson was that way. He threw a hissy fit because they changed a lot of wording and mutilated and mangled his Declaration of Independence. But if you look at the Declaration that he wrote and the final draft, it basically says the same thing, it's just that the prose is a little different.[53]

That's the compromise that's inherent in the legislative process by design. But filmmaking—Kubrick said that if you make only one compromise a day, by the end of your film you've made 300 compromises. How far will you go before you take that long walk down the road?

---

53 Three weeks earlier, I had sent John's assistant, Leonard Brady, a copy of Jefferson's original text of the Declaration of Independence with changes noted.

Kubrick was one who had enough money and enough time to do it and was treated better than anybody in the history of film. He was Stanley Kubrick and he got to live on the moors and do what he wanted and they used to say, "Just show us the film when you're done, Stanley." He isn't a good person to talk about. Kubrick fought his battles with neatly dressed regiments, with the finest equipment, total logistical support, being able to pick the ground and the time and the place, and usually the enemy. I have fought all my battles as a guerilla fighter—at night, with no or little ammunition, weapons that were stolen, and usually having to fall back after fighting against superior forces and try to hit them in places and get away with stuff because that was the only way it could be done. I learned much more from reading Mao and Geronimo and Victorio or Che Guevara than I did from reading about how Stanley Kubrick made things.

If you were a Liberal would you have had a longer and more productive career in Hollywood?

Certainly. I would have been less of a threat to western civilization. I've always been on the other side of the cultural war.

Some of the greatest films that have ever been made have been made by people with your beliefs.

Some of the greatest victories in military history were by people who certainly didn't have picked regiments. You can't sit there and say, "I want it this way! This is my vision! I must have it this way or I can't do it at all!" Because it becomes endless. First of all, you have to know what you want to do. Most filmmakers don't. Most filmmakers just want to be famous, they want people to say, "Oh, gosh, you're a director, you have the hat and the vest and the finder." And they don't care about the movies, they just want a big Hollywood movie with stars and lots of action in it, so they can get another job so they can be big Hollywood directors. They don't particularly care what the movie says or does; they don't start out with that. They talk about "their vision." They really don't have any vision. Some of those guys can make movies perfectly well. Movies don't have to all be done by *auteurs*. Some of the movies that are most celebrated by those who espouse the *auteur* theory are not particularly well-liked.

If you had to describe your vision—oh, God, this sounds like a People magazine question—what would it be?

I like personal films. I like John Ford because I like John Ford's sensibilities, aside from his skill. His skill is consummate. He's the best, most skilled of all directors. But I like his sentimentality, I like the things that he seems to care about. I like other directors often who are completely different because they're personal directors. Obviously I like Fellini because he's a personal director. There's a lot of Marty Scorsese's work that is good because of his personal feel.

Frank Capra, Leo McCarey, and you mentioned Delmer Daves.

Delmer Daves is one of my favorites. That's the kind of film I like the best, though sometimes there are films that are not personal, but are so experiential that they're good too. They take you to another place by sheer ability of the filmmaker to make you go through something. And I can't say that it all has to be serious, because some of the most satisfying films are not real serious. I personally like just about any Elvis film. I would think that *Viva Las Vegas* (George Sidney, 1964) is real high on my list of all time bests. The combination of the King and Ann-Margret, you can do no wrong. The King, Ann-Margret, and Vegas! It's one of the high points of the Twentieth Century (laughs).

If a true artist can make art about what he knows, and the writer is told to write what he knows, how do you place yourself and your sensibilities in different eras that you could not have lived through?

All of life adds up into the experience, and if people don't live life, but just look at movies, then they're going to make movies about movies, and the experiences that they saw in movies. That's what happens largely a lot of the time now; my generation was so influenced by movies that they take scenes from movies and re-do them, and they have sensibilities that totally come from movies, not from real life. Only so much comes from real life; everybody lives life; everybody has views of things. But only so much. Perhaps it should be like Larry McMurtry said, that we should be granted a tax allowance for depletion, the way oil people are. Because you're going to lose a certain amount in time. That's what happens a lot of the time now. When I was 17 years old I wanted to come home from Colorado, so I had to ride the freight train. While I was on the freight train with bums, real hobos, this guy told me that joke. He told me, "A guy goes to Alaska looking for work and someone asks him, 'Can you skin a bear?' He says, 'Sure, I can skin anything.' And the other fella says, 'Stay right there.' He goes and gets a grizzly bear to run in the room after him and he says, 'Skin that and I'll get you another.'" I never heard that joke again, but many years later I put it in *Jeremiah Johnson* where Bear Claw (Will Geer) takes Johnson to a cabin and then goes to get him a grizzly bear. Now, there's only so many of those things gonna happen to you. You're only gonna have so many jokes about grizzly bears being skinned.

If you hadn't been on a freight train, but had been home watching video tape—

—I wouldn't have had that experience. Because that was not a common joke that was being told to everybody. It wasn't being passed around the beach, it wasn't being told on television. That was something that I found that was a little gem of a piece of humanity in my travels. They were more extraordinary travels than normal, so I was gonna find a more extraordinary joke.

If you look at the early great filmmakers, they were the ones who had had a life before they started making movies. Whereas today they grow up with movies—

The whole thing is to be young, which is why so many movies are made about high school. Because that's the only life they have prior to making movies.

It's also the demographics of who goes to movies.

That used to be a dirty word—you never wanted to say, "I'm making my movie so it'll be like this or like that, and it'll fit to this audience, and they'll like it." It used to be that you were an artist breaking new ground. Now it's completely the opposite: the more you can make it key to a particular audience where you can manipulate it, the better you are. What you have to do to be a good filmmaker is to make stuff that is totally original and totally your take on the world, and if it's interesting enough and people go see it, they'll ask you to make another. That's the risk you take, like drilling for oil. If it isn't there, it's a dry hole, and you may have to find another way to make a living.

How do you feel about these interviews? About examining yourself and your work in this kind of detail?

When you read an interview with somebody, I want to know what the purpose of it is. What do you get out of it?

But sometimes, you see, it's the journey, and not the destination.

When I read interviews with screenwriters, I find that most of them are very arrogant. They love to tell you how great their work is—

If you're speaking the truth, you're not being arrogant.

— I don't feel I come off as arrogant. I come off as very strongly opinionated and very set in my ways. But not arrogant. I am an anachronism. It's pretty hard to be arrogant if you're an anachronism.

Afterword

We finished our interviews in October 2001 in the shadow of the terrorist attacks on America a month earlier. In the course of that month, Warner Bros, as did other studios, went into paranoid lockdown. Those that gave studio tours canceled them. Cars were searched entering as well as leaving the lots. And yet it was sadly comical; at Warner's Olive Avenue Gate 4, studio security parked a police car as a signal of readiness. Except it was a prop; not only did it never have a driver, it sat there day and night, rain and dry, collecting dust.

Less frivolous was a call John received from a low-level Hollywood producer (whom I knew and detested). This man had somehow finagled a grant from Uncle Sam to assemble a team of well-known action filmmakers into a think tank that would spitball outlandish terrorist plots as a cockeyed way to inspire the government's counter-terrorism program, presumably in case the experts hadn't already thought of them. Perhaps smelling a rat (he gave no specifics), John declined to participate. He has since done some legitimate consulting for the government.

When John had his stroke in July 2010, he was in New York with his friend, John Plaster (U.S. Army Special Forces, Retired). The two Johns, avid Mongologists, were researching Milius's long-dreamed-about Genghis Khan project. They had just finished dinner, a meal that the burly Milius always enjoyed. They were on their way to the car when Milius stopped in the middle of a sentence and fell silent. When Plaster asked him what was wrong, there was no response. Plaster immediately called 9-1-

1. By chance, an ambulance was ten minutes away and it took Milius to the nearest hospital E.R.

The first thing doctors determined was that he had lost his power of speech. What could not be known at that point was how much of the mind behind it might also be destroyed. He had just turned sixty-six.

It was a shock to his fellow filmmakers, those movie brats of the "New Hollywood" who had stormed the studios when they got out of cinema school and changed the course of the American film industry. Said Steven Spielberg, "I can't think of a worse thing ever happening to a person I knew...one of the greatest raconteurs of my generation...losing the ability to speak. It's the worst thing that's ever happened to any of my friends." To help him recover, Spielberg sent Milius a then-new invention called an iPad that made it possible for him to communicate through spelling and to refocus his mind for the rocky road back.

Milius had been in unwilling eclipse since the 1997 release of his TV movie, *Rough Riders*. Although he had been involved with the *Medal of Honor: European Assault* video game, his feature film career has stalled, and it was at that testy time that we conducted the bulk of the career interview in this book.

What kept him going was something I could not mention in the first, much-abridged version (which wasn't published until 2006): he had just pitched a series to HBO that would eventually start airing in 2005. It was *Rome*, and it not only shattered viewing records for the prestigious premium cable network, it inspired them to embark on additional series such as *Game of Thrones*, *Westworld*, *Perry Mason*, and others that have reshaped the cable and streaming industries. John's pitch for the series was smart and concise: *The Sopranos*[54] set in ancient Rome.

That was the good part. The bad part was that, despite that success, progress on his other projects ceased. In 2001, he discovered that his friend and accountant, Charles "Chuck"

---

54 *The Sopranos* ran on HBO from 1999 to 2007

Reidy, Jr., had been embezzling his assets, including his children's trust funds. It was more than a crime, it was a personal betrayal.[55] Producer-writer David Milch fronted John the money for son Ethan's law school tuition (which John paid back).

During this period, the Miliuses moved to a seacoast town not far from Boston where John lived the romantic life of a Hollywood exile (except without the romance, only the exile). It was his Elba.

"It would be nice to retire to someplace like that and teach," he once mused about liberal New England, "but those are all politically correct schools, and I don't think that I would last a day at one of those places. I'm a victim of my times; I don't fit in at all any more. Years ago I would've had it made. Now I'll probably be an outlaw till the day I die."

The New England adventure didn't last. He and his wife Elan would move to Sherman, New York, then to Millbrook, New York, where he rented a cabin in nearby Pine Plains to write. After his stroke, his marriage broke up.

In 2013, the documentary *Milius*, produced with love and skill by Zak Knutson and Joey Figueroa of Chop Shop Entertainment was shown in America on the Epix cable network. John attended its premiere at USC on January 9 of that year. Still recovering from his stroke, he was warmed by greetings from old friends and accepted the adoration of the audience with noblesse oblige. As we walked together afterward, he proudly disclosed to me that he was back at work on the 2009 Genghis Khan script and had attracted producer interest. (The project is in active development and financing at this writing.)

King Conan: Crown of Iron had a different odyssey. Milius wrote his official sequel (ignoring *Conan the Destroyer*, 1984, and *Red Sonja*, 1985) with a view to having Arnold Schwarzenegger reprise his original role as the regal Cimerian once the actor wrapped his then-current starring role as California's

---

55 From 1990 to 2001 Riedy had been drawing cash from Milius's investment accounts as sham payments for collectible firearms and transferred money from the Milius children's trust funds to cover his embezzlement. Charged in November, 2001, Riedy was tried and jailed, where he died in 2004.

Governor in 2007 when he would be sixty. In the story, Conan has made an unholy alliance with the Emperor to secure peace for his people in exchange for giving up his son, Kon, to the Emperor. Made restless and uncomfortable by this political contrivance, Conan grows lax in his rule. The script articulated Milius's long-held belief that true leaders should give up the throne before the legend is replaced by the reality of decrepit ageing. Written while he was enjoying the sponsorship of producer Joel Silver, Milius was apparently never considered as director. Instead, Robert Rodriguez (*From Dusk Till Dawn*, *Spy Kids*) was named director after Warner Bros. acquired the property (the *Conan* films were originally produced by Dino DeLaurentiis for Universal). When Rodriguez dropped out, the project was handed to the Wachowski siblings who had scored with *The Matrix*. Fans of both Conan and Milius knew that this did not bode well. In early 2004, Lilly Wachowski announced that she and her sister Lana had lost interest in the project and (thankfully) abandoned it. Finally, in 2011, Marcus Nispel remade *Conan the Barbarian* with Jason Momoa from a script by Thomas Dean Donnelly & Joshua Oppenheimer and Sean Hood,[56] Warner Bros. having had let go of the rights to Lionsgate. The new script was based on the Robert E. Howard tales, not the Milius-Stone screenplay. There were nineteen producers aboard, and one of them offered Arnold Schwarzenegger the token role of Corin, Conan's father (played in the original by William Smith). Schwarzenegger passed. When the remake failed at the box office, all planned sequels were called off.

A 2012 remake of *Red Dawn* was directed by Dan Bradley from a script by Carl Ellsworth and Jeremy Passmore based on the 1984 script by Milius and Kevin Reynolds. Where the original concerned a Russian invasion of America's heartland, the remake made the invaders Chinese until rights-holders MGM and United Artists suggested to the producers that the Chinese market was too important to slight by making them

---

[56] Milius's original screenplay, written with Oliver Stone, was not used. The screenwriters went to the Howard originals.

the bad guys, so the villains became North Korean (the Russians having by then become America's "friends"). Milius was not involved.

Nevertheless, he remains newsworthy. Fans such as author Pat Jankiewicz continue the debate over who wrote the Indianapolis speech in *Jaws* (*Just When You Thought It Was Safe: A Jaws Companion*, GA: Bear Manor Media, 2015); *Apocalypse Now: The Final Cut* (2919) revived interest in his work; and surfing groups constantly show *Big Wednesday*.

The February 10, 2019 death of *Big Wednesday*'s Jan-Michael Vincent brought Milius to Duke's restaurant in Malibu on April 24 -- naturally it was a Wednesday -- for a memorial to "Matt Johnson." Costars Lee Purcell, William Katt, Gary Busey and others attended.

"Milius was a center of attention on Wednesday night," affectionately wrote *Deadline Hollywood* reporter Mike Cieply. "Chris Kobin, who helped organize the event and featured Milius in the documentary *Hollywood Don't Surf!*, of which Kobin was a producer, stayed out of the limelight as one guest after another–Jeff Berg, Gary Busey, Billy Katt–paid court at the Milius table. And there he was, grizzled as ever, working somewhat to overcome the effects of a stroke he suffered in 2010, and wearing a bright red cap that said *Make Surfing Great Again*. Clearly, he is still at odds with his industry, his era, the prevailing political winds–with almost everything except for that very short time when, like his avatars in *Big Wednesday*, he lived on and for the beach."

Appropriately noting, "in a digital world, Milius remains an analog man," Cieply cited one of John's reactionary quotes by saying, "sentiment of that sort can bring banishment in the age of social media. Yet he was still standing proud as of Wednesday, the same John Milius. Crusty. Weathered. More than a bit damaged. But still real, and still unbowed. Mostly, he laughed, and repeated a few happy phrases, "Oh, yes, yes, yeah," and "very good!'

Afterword

Although I had interviewed him many times over nearly fifty years, our talks that inform this book began in 2000 when I was asked by Patrick McGilligan, editor of the *Backstory* series at the University of California Press, to sit down with John and chronicle his career. Understandably, the *Backstory* Q&A had to be cut for space lest it dominate the whole anthology; this Bear Manor edition is the first time that the restored, complete, preferred version, including updates, has appeared. Preparing for it, in late September 2020 I visited John in the condo in which he now lives in Brentwood in West Los Angeles. It is furnished in traditional style with walls festooned with photographs of his adventures (Desert Storm, surfing, hunting). The living room is guarded by a three-foot-tall sculpture of Arnold Schwarzenegger in his raised-sword pose from the Conan poster. It was a gift from Schwarzenegger and took two delivery men to carry it in. Significantly, there is not a single movie poster present, as if to state, "I have a life beyond movies."

His world now moves at a different pace. Living independently, he relaxes on his balcony overlooking a courtyard where neighbors greet him as if paying obeisance to a sovereign. Friends such as Francis Coppola and Jeff berg visit him there. His close friend of many years, actress/theatre producer Jeanette Driver, assists him in his everyday activities, shares his life, and helps him communicate.

The effects of the stroke will not be reversed. Jeanette has narrowed the diagnoses to Broca's aphasia and apraxia in that John's mind is sharp and unaffected, but getting the words from his brain to his mouth is a struggle, as is dealing with things told to him too rapidly or with background noise. Naturally, as we sat puffing cigars (I hadn't smoked a cigar all century, but would you turn down the chance to smoke a Cuban with John Milius?), a gardener's leaf blower kept overpowering our discourse.

There was another component to the stroke. John's right side was slightly weakened, but not so much that he can't still go out shooting with friends. That pleasure was on hold, however, because of Covid-19 sequestering. Indeed, he, Jeanette, and I were careful to sit six feet apart from one another, making the noisy leaf blower even more of a nuisance. And yet, despite all he had gone through, it may have been the most relaxed conversation we've had in years.

As I was leaving, the last scene from one of his first scripts, *Jeremiah Johnson*, crossed my mind. By the end of the story, Johnson (Robert Redford), the mountain man, has lost his wife and son, has nearly been killed by a bear, has fought dozens of Crow Indians, and has somehow survived. He is cooking a rabbit over a fire in the snow when his mentor, Bear Claw (Will Geer), comes upon him. "You come far, Pilgrim," Bear Claw says. "Were it worth the trouble?" As I stood to leave, I asked John the same thing. He looked at me with the same expression Redford used and said, as Johnson did, "Huh? What trouble?"

That's John. When all is said and done, what's left to say and do?

Appendix A: Filmography
(as writer-director unless otherwise noted):

"Marcello, I'm So Bored" (animated short; John Strawbridge, co-creator, 1967)
"Glut" (Basil Pouledoris, 1967)(writer and casting)
"Viking Women Don't Care" (Caleb Deschanel, 1967)(weapons advisor)
"The Emperor" (George Lucas, 1967)(crew)
Devil's 8 (Burt Topper, 1969) (co-screenplay)
Evel Knievel (Marvin Chomsky, 1971)
Dirty Harry (Donald Siegel, 1971) (uncredited contribution)
The Life and Times of Judge Roy Bean (John Huston, 1972)
Jeremiah Johnson (Sydney Pollack, 1972)(co-screenplay)
Dillinger (1973)
Magnum Force (Ted Post, 1973)(story; co-screenplay)
Melvin Purvis: G-Man (Dan Curtis, 1974)(story)(TV)
The Wind and the Lion (1975)
Jaws (1975) (uncredited contribution)
Big Wednesday (1978)(co-screenplay)
Apocalypse Now (Francis Coppola, 1979)(co-screenplay)
1941 (Steven Spielberg, 1979)(co-story)
Hardcore (Paul Schrader, 1979)(executive producer)
Conan the Barbarian (1982)(co-screenplay)
Uncommon Valor (Ted Kotcheff, 1983)(executive producer)
Lone Wolf McQuade (Steve Carver, 1983) (spiritual advisor and uncredited contribution)
Red Dawn (1984)(co-screenplay)
The Twilight Zone: Opening Day (1985) TV (directed only)
Extreme Prejudice (Walter Hill, 1987)(co-story; original script not used)
Farewell to the King (1989)
Flight of the Intruder (1990)(directed; uncredited rewrite)
The Hunt for Red October (John McTiernan, 1990)(uncredited contribution)
Geronimo: An American Legend (Walter Hill, 1993)(script)
Clear and Present Danger (Philip Noyce, 1994)(co-script)
Motorcycle Gang (1994)TV (directed only)
Rough Riders (1997) TV
Texas Rangers (2000)(Steve Miner) (removed name)
Rome (2005) TV co-creator
Between the Lines: The True Story of Surfers and the Vietnam War (2008) (guest writer)
Red Dawn (2012)(1984 screenplay)

Notable Awards: Winner, National Student Film Award, "Marcello, I'm So Bored", 1967; Academy Award® nomination, Apocalypse Now, 1979

Appendix B: Exact Screen and Presskit Credits:

Devil's 8 (1969)
Directed by Burt Topper
Story by Larry Gordon
Screenplay by Willard Huyck, John Milius, James Gordon White

Evel Knievel (1971)
Directed by Marvin J. Chomsky
Screen Play by Alan Calilou and John Milius
Story by Alan Calilou

Jeremiah Johnson (1972)
Directed by Sydney Pollack
Screenplay by John Milius and Edward Anhalt
Based upon the novel *Mountain Man* by Vardis Fisher
and the story "Crow Killer" by Raymond W. Thorp and Robert Bunker

The Life and Times of Judge Roy Bean (1972)
Directed by John Huston
Original Screenplay by John Milius

Magnum Force (1973)
Directed by Ted Post
Screenplay by John Milius and Michael Cimino
Story by John Milius
Based on original material by Harry Julian Fink and R. M. Fink

Dillinger (1973)
Written and Directed by John Milius

Melvin Purvis: G-Man (1974)
Directed by Dan Curtis
Created by John Milius
Teleplay by John Milius and William F. Nolan
Story by John Milius

The Wind and the Lion (1975)
Written and Directed by John Milius

Big Wednesday (1978)
Directed by John Milius
Written by John Milius & Dennis Aaberg

Appendix B: Exact Screen and Presskit Credits

Apocalypse Now (1979)
Directed by Francis Coppola
Written by John Milius and Francis Coppola
Narration by Michael Herr

1941 (1979)
Directed by Steven Spielberg
Screenplay by Robert Zemeckis & Bob Gale
Story by Robert Zemeckis & Bob Gale and John Milius

Hardcore (1979)
Written and Directed by Paul Schrader
Executive Producer John Milius

Used Cars (1980)
Directed by Robert Zemeckis
Screenplay by Robert Zemeckis & Bob Gale
Executive Producers Bob Gale, John Milius, Steven Spielberg and John G. Wilson

Uncommon Valor (1983)
Directed by Ted Kotcheff
Written by Joe Gayton
Produced by John Milius and Buzz Feitshans

Conan the Barbarian (1982)
Written by John Milius and Oliver Stone
Based on the Character Created by Robert E. Howard

Red Dawn (1984)
Screenplay by Kevin Reynolds and John Milius
Story by Kevin Reynolds

Twilight Zone: Opening Day (1985)
Directed by John Milius
Written by Chris Hubbell and Gerrit Graham

Extreme Prejudice (1987)
Directed by Walter Hill
Story by John Milius and Fred Rexer
Screenplay by Deric Washburn and Harry Kleiner

Farewell to the King (1989)
Written for the Screen and Directed by John Milius
Based on the novel *L'Adieu Au Roi* by Pierre Schoendoerffer

Flight of the Intruder (1990)
Directed by John Milius
Screenplay by Robert Dillon and David Shaber
Based on the Novel by Stephen Coonts

Geronimo: An American Legend (1993)
Story by John Milius
Screenplay by John Milius and Larry Gross

Clear and Present Danger (1994)
Directed by Philip Noyce
Based on the Novel by Tom Clancy
Screenplay by Donald Stewart and Steven Zaillian and John Milius

Motorcycle Gang (1994)
Directed by John Milius
Written by Kent Anderson and Laurie McQuillin
Story by Kent Anderson

Rough Riders (1997)
Directed by John Milius
Written by John Milius and Hugh Wilson

Appendix C:
Unrealized/Pending Projects

Dates refer to most recent draft. Unless noted as a collaboration, Milius is the sole credited writer (partial list).

Night Drop (1984)
Research for proposed Stanley Kubrick project about a daring Allied airborne deployment immediately prior to D-Day, 1944.

China Marines (1985)
Milius would direct (and possibly rewrite) from Eric Strahl's script.

Daniel Boone (1992)
Historically accurate saga of the eastern woodsman who opened up the American west, paying full respect to Native Americans.

The Northmen (1993-1999)
Perennially in-preparation Viking project written with Randall McCormick.

Sgt. Rock (1993-1997)
Based on DC Comics' WW2 series with Arnold Schwarzenegger as the solid Sergeant of Easy Company, plus Bruce Willis and Sylvester Stallone under Ridley Scott's direction.

Secret Smile (1995)
Screenplay by Steven Seagal; rewrite by Milius and Seagal.

Mistress of the Seas (1995)
Original screenplay in the Joseph Conrad mode.

Without Remorse (1995)
Adaptation of Tom Clancy novel about a Navy S.E.A.L. who goes to Vietnam looking for evidence of P.O.W.s.

Cortes (1996)
Sweeping tale of Hernando Cortes's conquest of Mexico. Written with Werner Herzog.

Wanted: Dead or Alive (1996)
Not to be confused with the 1987 Rutger Hauer update of the classic Steve McQueen TV show.

Asia Pacific (1999)
Television series. Pilot episode titled "Whistling at the Cobra" written with Dan Gagliasso.

Manila John (1999)
Television series.

The Thirty (1999)
Feature film.

Patriotism (nee M.A.D.: The Life and Times of Curtis LeMay, a.k.a. LeMay) (2000)
Free-swinging biography of maverick U.S. Army general.

The Greatest Raid of All (2000)
Co-screenplay with John Plaster about the secret U.S. *Son Tay* raid into North Vietnam.

King Conan (2000)
See Afterword

Genghis Kahn (2009)
Epic story of the great Mongol conqueror

Appendix D: Bear's Big Wednesday Speech

Setting: The novelization is slightly different from the script, which didn't make the final cut. The raucous party at Mrs. Barlow's house is petering out. Matt, Leroy, Jack, Sally, Boogie, ands Chubby cluster around Bear, the experienced surfer who makes all their boards and tells them stories.[57]

"Boogie, give me another beer. It may not be the same. It changes each time I tell it. . .

"Well, back in Hawaii, there was a small group of us that first used to ride big waves on the north shore. We were a crazy bunch of bastards -- fools. We rode places no one had ever ridden before. Sometimes things got really hairy. We were a strange breed. When we rode Waimea the first time, Simmons was quoting Yates in the lineup.

"Anyway, the day you wanta hear about was in '58. It was Woody Brown and another guy. They were best friends. A friend meant a lot to you then, especially when it was only the two of you in big water. Woody and his friend were riding Sunset Beach. Nobody knew much about Sunset then. It was getting late and the waves were running about ten to twelve. The sun was almost down when it started to happen.

"A huge set started to build on the horizon. The lines, long and black, must have been eighteen to twenty feet. They paddled for their lives.

"Up -- up the first waves. They cleared easily but the next waves were bigger. They paddled over these and from the tops of them they could see no end to the set -- just towering black walls shutting out the horizon.

They paddled over waves twenty-five to thirty feet high. Waves bigger than anyone had ever been in -- out past the lineup. The whole coast was closed out. The water churned

[57] *Big Wednesday* by John Milius and Dennis Aaberg (NY: Bantam Books, 1978)

with black rivers from the riptides. They had no choice but to paddle down to Waimea where there might be a chance to get in. Waves were hitting the cliff and splashing a hundred feet.

"They were tired when that set came. I don't know how big it was. They paddled up over wave after wave, thirty-five to forty feet high. Death waves.

"Woody couldn't take it anymore. His arms had turned to rope. He turned to his friend and said, 'Fuck it, let's drown.'

"His friend was tired, too. He didn't care if he died either and so he didn't stop Woody when he spun around and took off on that wave. The friend paddled out to sea in the middle of the night. It was pitch black and he was paddling over sixty-foot waves and could hear them break behind. The Coast Guard found him the next morning, two miles off shore, out of his mind."

Bear stopped and took a long drink. Sally looked puzzled.

"What about the other one? The one that rode?" asked Sally.

"His friend should have made him go on. They never found Woody. Never found his body. Just pieces of his board."

"Big Wednesday, 1958, eh Bear?" Chubby said reverently.

"Yeah, well, it always happens on Wednesday. Come on, Boogie, play another song."

NAT SEGALOFF Biography

Nat Segaloff is a writer-producer-journalist. He has variously been a studio publicist, college teacher, broadcaster, and newspaperman. He is the author of twenty books including *Hurricane Billy: The Stormy Life and Films of William Friedkin, Arthur Penn: American Director,* and *Final Cuts: The Last Films of 50 Great Directors* in addition to career monographs on Stirling Silliphant, Walon Green, Paul Mazursky and John Milius (of which this book is an expanded and updated iteration). His writing has appeared in such varied periodicals as *Film Comment, Written By, International Documentary, Animation Magazine, The Christian Science Monitor, Time Out* (US), *MacWorld,* and *American Movie Classics Magazine.* He was also senior reviewer for AudiobookCafe.com and contributing writer to *Moving Pictures* magazine. His *The Everything® Etiquette Book* and *The Everything Trivia Book* and *The Everything® Tall Tales, Legends & Outrageous Lies Book* were published by Adams Media Corp.

Nat is the co-author of *The Waldorf Conference* (with Daniel M. Kimmel and Arnie Reisman) a comedy-drama about the secret meeting of studio moguls that began the Hollywood Blacklist, which had its all-star world premiere at L.A. Theatre Works. and was acquired for production by Warner Bros. He was staff producer for The Africa Channel, wrote the stage comedy *Closets* (produced at Massachusetts' Gloucester Stage Company), and was writer for the popular public radio quiz show "Says You!" after having been a frequent guest panelist.

Other books include *A Lit Fuse: The Provocative Life of Harlan Ellison* (NESFA Press), nominated for Hugo and Locus awards, and, for Bear Manor Media, *Stirling Silliphant: The Fingers of God; Mr. Huston/Mr. North: Life, Death, and the Making of John Huston's Last Film; Screen Saver: Private Stories of*

Public Hollywood and its sequel, *Screen Saver Too: Hollywood Strikes Back, Guiding Royalty: My Adventure with Elizabeth Taylor and Richard Burton* (co-written with Yoram Ben-Ami), and *Guarding Gable*. More recently for Bear Manor he wrote *Hollywood & Venal*, a collection of "stories with a secret" originally written for Nikki Finke's celebrated Hollywood Dementia® website (illustrated by Thomas Warming), and the second edition of *Arthur Penn: American Director*.

Nat lives in Los Angeles waiting for his phone calls to be returned.

Acknowledgments

Thanks to Mike Cieply, Ethan Harari, Matt Luber, and André Morgan for help updating this manuscript. Earlier thanks to Patrick McGilligan, Walt von Hoffe, Christopher Darling, and Milt Moritz of American International Pictures who believed me in my press agent days when I said I could get publicity for John in Boston.

Special thanks are reserved for Leonard Brady, John's indefatigable assistant during the time these talks took place, and to Jeanette Driver, who is now devoted to John.

Deepest appreciation to artist Thomas Warming who not only captured the man's films in his extraordinary cover illustration but the man himself.

Continuing gratitude, of course, to Ben Ohmart of Bear Manor Media whose love of film cannot be overstated.

Index

1941, 61

A
Aaberg, Dennis 45, 46, 47, 50, 156, 160
Academy of Motion Picture Arts and Sciences 127, 154
Achilles 35, 67, 128
Alphonse XIII hotel, Spain 41
America (as theme) 43, 70, 72, 101, 104, 147, 149
Ann-Margret 143
Apache 94, 106
Apocalypse Now 55, 56, 58-61, 66, 71, 74, 99, 127, 128, 151, 154, 156
Arthurian legend 46
asthma (John's) 3, 4, 13, 94

B
Baldwin, Alec 115
Barlow, Jack 44, 45, 50, 99, 160
Barwood, Hal 9
Bean, Judge Roy 23, 26, 27, 29, 30, 78, 117, 154, 155
Bear (Sam Melville) 19, 28, 46, 48, 54, 122, 123, 144, 151-153, 160-164
Beatty, Warren 75
Benton, Robert 38, 127
Beowulf 65
Berenger, Tom 101, 102
Berg, Jeff 151, 152
Bergen, Candace 39
Bergman, Ingmar 130
Bergman, Sandahl 168
Big Wednesday 44-48, 50-54, 71, 88, 96, 99, 120, 121, 127, 151, 154, 155, 160, 161
Bond, James Bond 113
Boothe, Powers 71, 73, 107
Borneo 20, 93, 94
Brady, Leonard 141, 164

Brando, Marlon 58
Busey, Gary 44, 88, 151

C
Capra, Frank 128, 143
Carpenter, John 9
Carson, Lance 45, 47, 50
Carver, Steve ix
Chomsky, Marvin 154, 155
Cici (John Husrton's wife) 31
Cieply, Mike 151, 164
Cimino, Michael 155
Clancy, Tom 109, 115, 157, 158
Clear and Present Danger 108. 108, 112,.119
Conan the Barbarian 64-69, 85, 93, 129, 149, 150, 152, 154, 156, 159
Connery, Sean 39, 41, 61, 71
Coppola, Francis Ford 42, 55, 58, 135, 152, 154, 156

D
Dafoe, Willem 98, 120
Daves, Delmer 143
DeLaurentiis, Dino 64, 65, 68, 69, 150
Deschanel, Casleb 154
Devil's 8 13, 14, 154, 155
DiCaprio, Leonardo 18
dick, John Dillinger's 36
Dillinger, John viii, 33-38, 53, 71, 94, 113, 117, 154, 155
Dirty Harry 13, 17, 18, 21, 23-26, 30, 61, 98, 103, 133, 145, 154
Dreyfuss, Richard 34
Driver, Jeanette 152, 153, 164
Durendal (sword) 49
D'Arbanville, Patti 49

E
Eastwood, Clint 17, 18, 22, 23, 26, 62

Index

Englund, Robert 45
Extreme Prejudice 70, 105-106

F
Farewell to the King, x, 90-96, 119, 139
Feitshans, Buzz 156
Figueroa, Joey 149
Flight of the Intruder 119, 197-198
Ford, John 38, 53-55, 75, 76, 100, 109, 114, 115, 135, 143

G
Gable, Clark 28, 163
Geronimo 106, 107, 142, 154, 157
Gierash, Stefan 19
Glut, Donald 9, 11, 154

H
Hamilton, George 32, 78
Hawks, Howard 75, 118
Hill, Walter 30, 100, 103, 106, 117, 154, 156
Hoover, J. Edgar 36
Hopalong Cassidy (William Boyd) 8
Hudson, Bob "Emperor" 12, 77
Hunt for Red October 70, 60, 108
Huston, John 27, 28, 30, 31, 41, 141, 154, 155, 162
Huyck, Willard 9, 13, 139, 155

J
Jan-Michael 44, 47, 50, 52, 88, 151
Jaster (dog) 28
Jaws 24, 42, 60, 151, 154
Jeremiah Johnson 16-20, 25, 71, 78, 107, 144, 153-155

K
Kael, Pauline 25
Kakela, Wayne 5, 8
Kanaly, Steve 35
Katt, William 44, 88, 151
Kazanjian, Howard 9
Keith, Brian 40, 102

Kershner, Irvin 21, 22
Knievel, Bobby "Evel" 19, 32, 33, 78, 154, 155
Knutson, Zak 149
Kubrick, Stanley 40, 129, 141, 142, 158
Kurosawa, Akira 51

L
Lancaster, Burt 22
Langry, Lily 27
Lean, David 30, 41, 91
Learoyd 91, 92, 94-97
LeMay, General Curtis 89, 111, 121, 123, 126, 159
Life and Times of Judge Roy Bean 26, 116
Locke, Sondra 26
Lone Wolf McQuade ix
Lopez, Gerry 48, 49, 53, 71, 75, 97
Lucas, George 9, 12, 15, 42, 55, 77, 154

M
MacArthur, General Douglas 134, 135
Magnum Force 23
Mako 93
Malick, Terrence 21, 23
"Marcello I'm So Bored" 10, 11, 15, 154
Medavoy, Mike 15, 16
Milius, Amanda (daughter)(xii
Milius, Celia (second wife) Celia 45
Milius, Ethan (son) xii, 149
Milius, John 2, 9, 10, 13, 17, 18, 27, 34, 39, 44, 55, 58, 64, 66, 70, 77-79, 86, 88, 89, 91, 98, 100, 106, 116, 126, 131, 147-152, 155-158, 160, 162
Milius, Marcus (son) xii
Milius, Renee (Fabri, first wife) xii
Milius, William Styx (father) 2, 4, 11, 29, 67, 79, 102, 150
Muñoz, Mickey 6

N
narration of films 45, 116, 132, 156
Newman, Paul 27, 28, 38
Nolte, Nick 71, 85, 91, 92, 93, 107

Noyce, Philip 109, 154, 157

O
Oates, Warren 34
Oberon, Elan xii, 94, 149
O'Neal, Ron 74

P
Patton, General George S. 72, 130, 135
Paulettes (critic Pauline Kael sycophants) 25
Peckinpah, Sam 17
Pedicaris, Eden/Ian 39-41
Pollack, Sydney 17, 18, 20, 107, 154, 155
Pontecorvo, Gillo 127
Posie (dog) x
Pouledoris, Basil 9, 154
Purvis, Melvin 34-36, 71, 154, 155

R
Raisuli/Raisuni 39-41, 71, 83
Rambo 131
Rayfiel, David 18
Red Dawn 53, 57, 70-76, 91, 114, 150, 154, 156
Redford, Robert 17, 18, 153
Rodriguez, Robert 150
Roosevelt, President Theodore 39, 40, 71, 79, 80, 85, 100-103
Rough Riders 99-104, 116, 119, 125, 147
Runyon, Damon 36, 37

S
Sandburg, Carl 19
Schoendoerffer, Pierre 91, 93, 157
Schrader, Paul 154, 156
Schwarzenegger, Arnold 64, 85, 149, 150, 152, 158
Scorsese, Martin 15, 58
Spielberg, Steven 42, 51, 58, 60-62, 96, 127, 136, 148, 154, 156
Starkweather, Charles 35
Steinbeck, John 47, 138

Surfers and surfing 3, 6, 7, 11, 14, 44, 45, 47-49, 51-54, 77, 127, 139, 151-154, 160

U
Used Cars 60-61

V
Vikings 7, 11, 74, 112, 154, 158
Vincent, Jan-Michael 44, 47, 52, 88, 100, 151
voice-over, use of (see also narration) 116

W
Wachowski siblings 150
Wellman, William 75
Whiteman School 5, 8
Wind and the Lion, The vi, 37-42
writing 6, 8, 10, 12, 17, 18, 20, 22, 24, 26, 42, 55-58, 60, 62, 65, 98, 104, 106, 108, 110-112, 114, 119, 120, 123, 125, 137-140, 149, 162

Y
Yaeger 8

Z
Zaillian, Steve 113, 114, 157
Zemeckis, Robert 9, 61, 62, 156

Printed in Great Britain
by Amazon